YOU'RE GONNA MAKE IT AFTER ALL

The Life, Times and Influence of Mary Tyler Moore

New York Times Best-selling Author

MARC SHAPIRO

For more information contact:
Riverdale Avenue Books
5676 Riverdale Avenue
Riverdale, NY 10471.

www.riverdaleavebooks.com

Design by www.formatting4U.com
Cover by Scott Carpenter

Digital ISBN: 978-1-62601-410-7
Print ISBN: 978-1-62601-411-4

First Edition October, 2017

THIS BOOK IS DEDICATED TO:

All the people who, mentally, emotionally and in all other ways, get me up and off to my appointed rounds. As always, the brains and the beauty in the family, my wife Nancy. The extended family: Daughter Rachael, granddaughter Lily (who at age five is already fluent in English, Spanish and Grandpa). The latest in the fold, Brent, Robert and Layla…and lest I forget… Dave and Gloria. Super agent Lori Perkins is always in my corner. Brady, the designated man's best friend. All the great authors, musicians and artists who are constantly running through my head and finally the late and great Mary Tyler Moore who proved that it is possible to juggle fantasy and reality and not drop a thing.

TABLE OF CONTENTS

Author's Notes
Make It Different

There are no hard and fast rules in celebrity book publishing. I take that back; there are a couple.

Get it out first is a good rule to live by. Win, place and show only count in horse racing. Get it out reasonably fast is also right up there. You may have the better book but six months down the road, who is going to take the time to compare? But, bottom line and probably most important, tell a story that is insightful, entertaining, inspiring and, finally, totally different from anything that has ever been written about the subject. In which case, forget about the first two. Because positive word of mouth will take care of the rest.

The late and legendary actress Mary Tyler Moore is a case in point.

When Moore died on January 25, 2017 at age 80, she had spent untold decades in the public eye. Her stints on the iconic *The Dick Van Dyke Show* and *The Mary Tyler Moore Show*, her award winning turn in the major motion picture, *Ordinary People* and, yes, even those ultra cheesy *Happy Hotpoint* commercials made her a legendary actress and, to many, an important footnote in the women's movement.

But there was more, so much more, to the actress and her time. Her 1995 autobiography *After All* was a candid look at the reality of her life and her battles with alcoholism while in 2009, a second memoir entitled *Growing Up Again: Life, Love and Oh Yeah Diabetes*, talked at length and with much candor about her bout with the disease.

Bottom line, Moore had been upfront and public about pretty much everything, personal and professional, in her life. So I was somewhat surprised when my editor emailed me a couple of days after Moore's passing and wanted to know if I would like to do a book on the life of Mary Tyler Moore. I was more than interested.

Strong women almost always make for an interesting story. I've been up close and personal on a professional level with some of them for seemingly forever as editors, publicists, fellow writers and, of course, my agent. And one thing they've all had in common was the drive, the determination and the independent streak that drives us all to get the job done and get it done right. With rare exceptions, the women who have made history in any way, shape or form have never strayed far from the goal of professionalism and a dedication to garner respect through hard work and well thought out decisions. One need only have examined Mary Tyler Moore's life and times to recognize that she had long been a paid-up member of this exclusive club. She was not the type of person who is crying out for somebody to chronicle her life and times.

I was a lifelong fan and, as such, I was eminently qualified for the task.

I can honestly say I saw her very first film, a 1961 quickie opposite Charles Bronson called *X-15*. I remember seeing her opposite Elvis Presley in 1969 (in Germany no less) in a film called *Change of Habit*. I knew that she had posed for more than a dozen cheesecake record album covers in the 50's and early 60's. So yeah, I was in.

Until I mentally took stock and realized that there was really not that much new to talk about other than her final year of life. And I was not about to simply recycle old and familiar news. So, I took a step back and thought about it. And finally came up with an angle that was literally staring me in the face.

Which is that the life of Mary Tyler Moore was only a part of the story.

A lot was going on socially and politically in the actresses' world as Moore came of age and embarked on a successful career in Hollywood. Attitudes and morality were evolving and reforming into a sphere of new opportunities and possibilities for women and Moore's ascension as first an actress and later a producer and tastemaker of some influence were in direct confluence with this brave new world that was coming on strong. Mixing straightforward biography and how the changing world had or had not impacted Moore's life and career would be the way to go.

But there would be more to investigate. Yes, the actress was part and parcel of being on the cusp and a subtle driving force of, much that was going on in the women's movement. However, there was more to navigate than that. Above all, she was a human being whose life forced her into many personal and professional challenges, challenges that did not always lead to a positive outcome. That she would react in a certain way was a given. Internally, there was much in making those decisions that forced deep thinking and, by turns, a turning away from long held personal attitudes. Mary Tyler Moore, through thoughts and deeds, was much more than a flavor of the moment. This would not be happy talk strung together with silk and pretty flowers, admittedly much in keeping with her most well remembered performances in *The Dick Van Dyke Show* and *The Mary Tyler Moore Show*. That Mary Tyler Moore was out there, experiencing real life in a real world, often light years removed from the fantasy world of Hollywood, would provide industrial strength insights into just what made her tick.

My editor liked the idea and made a few suggestions on how to proceed. One thing we both agreed upon was that this would be a much deeper, thoughtful book than a mere by-the-numbers celebrity biography. These would not be the expected questions asked and dutifully answered. To do the life and times of Mary Tyler Moore, and to do it right, would entail more than crashing out the book in ten weeks. It would, to a large extent be two books, equal parts biography and history of a movement that may well have been instrumental in birthing a Mary Tyler Moore. Long story short, it would be different.

At the core of it all was research, lots of it and in a lot of different corners. The chronology of her credits and the more public and personal moments in her life were out there to be found. Tracking down people who knew her when would prove to be a more difficult proposition. When someone lives to be 80 the chances are good that a lot of people who knew her personally and professionally had already passed. But there were nuggets to be found, especially in the voices who would quickly proclaim that if it had not been for Moore, they would not have gone on to have the degrees of celebrity or just plain successful lives that they had achieved.

Everybody from television journalist Andrea Mitchell to rock and roller Joan Jett has admitted to owing a debt of gratitude to Moore. Oprah Winfrey? Tina Fey? Michelle Obama? They all have kind things to say. And it wasn't all clichés. There was reverence and a real sense of appreciation and honor to be following in Moore's footsteps.

One of the nagging questions in piecing Mary Tyler Moore's life and times together was, most certainly, her feminist leanings or lack thereof. It all depended on which stone was overturned. Some saw her as a shining example of where the women's movement was going, especially in popular culture of the late 60's into the mid 70's. Others saw her as an often reluctant target of the growing and often aggressive women's rights organizations. Still others saw her as the face of the moment who was, considered by many, to be a victim of timing, pure and simple. A lot of sweat equity would be invested in sorting it all out.

The reality would finally turn out to be that Mary Tyler Moore and the feminist movement were traveling similar paths but at somewhat different angles and for a fairly short period of time. Her work in *The Dick Van Dyke Show* made subtle, yet memorable inroads into the real world and the women's movement's drive for equality. But it would remain for *The Mary Tyler Moore Show*, and the advent of truly progressive thought in between the laughs that would, permanently, link Moore to the women's movement. Quite honestly, nothing Moore did after that show would have the impact of the little sitcom that could. And for better or worse, she would forever be Mary Richards.

From the outset, it was my intent to be judicious in quoting from Moore herself. This would not be a book heavy on set anecdotes and who she worked with and how they were or were not good people. Those bon mats were from another day and another book which told those kinds of stories. I was looking for moments for when the actress waxed, political, philosophical or spiritual and acknowledged an awareness of the world that was spinning around her.

There would be moments when the real issues and events of the feminist movement would appear, to form both an historical and, by degrees, educational perspective, on the evolving world that would inspire and effect Moore. I'd like to think that if she were around today, Moore would be thrilled to know some history and some facts that had gone hand in hand with her life and career.

Those expecting a largely chronological odyssey will get that. But there are moments where the whole story, out of necessity, doubles back on itself. Moore was faced with a myriad of professional and personal decisions that often tested her conscience, her upbringing and what the evolution of life experiences was teaching her.

How did the politics of the real world force her to think in and outside the box? Did she have an impact on society or was it the other way around? Moore was

America's sweetheart, that was a given. But how did that tag impact her for better or worse? Hence a more detailed chapter in which the actress deals with a singular situation might follow a chapter. Things that are often life lessons, often harshly learned, and the intestinal fortitude that saw her through those challenging nights into the light of day are up for consideration. What I would ultimately find was that, behind the fictional characters that captured our hearts and minds, was a real human being who had her real moments.

But don't worry, this book is not all gloom and doom. Who could not laugh at the notion of Moore posing for cheesecake photos for album covers of equally cheesy Cha-Cha music? And then there was Moore's role that was as far as one could get from Mary Richards' as a terrifying adoption agency head who was doing some truly unspeakable things on the side in the seldom seen and underappreciated movie for television called *Stolen Babies*. Moore was so good in this extreme change of pace that she snagged an Emmy for the role.

You're Gonna Make It After All: The Life, Times and Influence of Mary Tyler Moore is, at the end of the day, something old but definitely something new. It is a deep look into an entertaining and inspiring person who also knew the reality of the world around her. Hopefully, you'll find it is a very different take.

Marc Shapiro, 2017

Introduction
Break on Through

Mary Tyler Moore's working rights and the growing women's rights movement of the 1960's walked hand in hand through much of the decade.

The women's movement had its official, albeit low key, unveiling in 1961 when President John F. Kennedy launched with little fanfare and little in the way of progress, the Commission on the Status of Women. The movement would take on a much stronger presence in 1963 when Betty Friedan's ground breaking work *The Feminine Mystique*, laid out the first account of note on how unequal the men vs. women social and political status in this country truly was. That same year, journalist and growing feminist Gloria Steinem went undercover to audition to be a Playboy Bunny and emerged with a scathing account of low pay, sexual harassment and racism in the hallowed halls of Hugh Hefner's empire.

To break the shackles of low paying and limited options for women in the workplace was a driving force behind the 60's feminist movement. The credo of such early leaders in the feminist movement as Friedan and Steinem was that women should have more on their life's journey than wife, mother and homemaker; that women should be paid the same as men for doing the same job was a given.

And while Moore's struggles were played out on a more glamorous stage, her plight was seemingly similar. Her career in the 50's and early 60's had her playing along with Hollywood's version of the very thing the growing women's movement was fighting. From her earliest jobs as dancer and album cover cheesecake model, to bit parts in just about seemingly every show on television, Moore was alternately eye candy, obedient wife, mother, homemaker and various shades of 'It' girl. Easily her most infamous role, and in hindsight, a prime example of the male dominated Hollywood industry, was her first recurring role in the television series *Richard Diamond: Private Detective* in which Moore played the detective's sultry voiced receptionist Sam, a mystique which consisted of Moore seen only in shadow, except for her shapely legs.

The irony was that while *Richard Diamond: Private Detective* was pretty formula fare, the mysterious Sam quickly became the reason people tuned in. Moore, in a largely perceived feminist move, recognized her power on the show and immediately went to the Richard Diamond producers and strongly suggested that it was time for a raise in pay. The producers responded by firing Moore after 13 episodes and replacing her with another anonymous actress. For the actress, it would be, whether she realized it or not, her first feminist strike.

The feminist rebellion would continue on several fronts during the early to mid 60's, organizing into

The National Organization of Women (NOW) with Steinem becoming the de facto spokeswoman at marches, protests and symbolic bra burnings. In hushed corners, establishment types were cringing at the thoughts of women's sexual rights and the repercussions of 'the pill.'

And in her own subtle way, Moore was striking a blow for women's rights as it pertained to traditional television mores and dresses vs pants.

Call it sexist. Call it puritanical. But television in the late 50's and into the mid 60's seemed to be a seemingly antiquated place for women. Shows like *Ozzie & Harriet* and *Leave It to Beaver* pigeonholed women as wives and mothers. But what made these shows truly conspicuous was that no matter what mundane chore they were doing and no matter what time of day it was, they were uniformly wearing dresses and heels, more suited for a formal get together than doing the dishes or vacuuming the house.

Consequently, when Moore landed the role of loving wife and mother Laura Petrie in *The Dick Van Dyke Show*, it came as no surprise when her on set costume was the time honored dresses and heels. Moore, who by the 60's had already developed a reputation as a solid performer who rarely rocked the boat, unexpectedly dug in her heels.

"Wearing pants is what I do in real life," Moore insisted in a conversation with *Variety*. "It's what my friends do in real life and that's being a realistic wife who wears pants and does not care how she looks."

Moore took her complaint right to the top, in this case the show's creator Carl Reiner who, in turn, passed it on to the network. Her complaint, during a

TV Guide interview, continued to be "That women don't wear full skirted dresses to vacuum in."

"The network's response was that 'You know, we're afraid that housewives are going to be a little annoyed," she continued, "because she looks so good in pants." The show's sponsors, who typically were the final vote in any controversies were not fond of the look as reported in a *National Public Radio* conversation with Moore. "They said they were worried about the fit of the pants. What they really meant was that they were concerned about how the pants would fit my butt."

Finally a compromise was reached. Moore laughed when explaining the situation to *TV Guide*. "They made the show's creator Carl Reiner not to let her wear pants in more than one scene per episode. We went along with that for about three episodes. But within a few weeks we were sneaking more scenes of my wearing pants into more scenes in each episode. Finally it got to the point where I was just wearing pants all the time and everyone thought it was great. We got the absolution of men everywhere and women kind of breathed a sigh of relief and said 'Hey that's right. That's what we wear."

Moore would acknowledge in the aftermath of the pants controversy that a bit of history had been made. "Wearing pants on a popular sitcom definitely broke new ground," she told *National Public Radio*. And everyone thought it was great."

Given Moore's go with the flow middle American nature, her defiance of *The Dick Van Dyke Show* and, to a lesser degree her demanding a pay raise on *Richard Diamond Private Detective*, had put Moore on the radar of the burgeoning women's movement who was always on the lookout for spokeswomen who were celebrity in nature and in the public eye. By the late 60's, Moore and the feminist women's movement were making big strides. The National Organization of Women was making noticeable advances in the social, sexual and economic arenas and in many cases these strides were seen as shrill demands. In the meantime, it was hinted in the trades that Moore was about to embark on a new series, *The Mary Tyler Moore Show*, that would, simultaneously, kick open heretofore unheard of options in the real world for women.

Whether she liked it or not, Moore was suddenly being held in high regard in the growing women's movement and was being considered as a standard bearer for the voices that were now demanding to be heard. The reality of Moore's sudden recognition in the feminist world, quite simply, depended on who one talked to. For Jennifer Keishin Armstrong, an author and pop culture maven whose book *Mary And Lou And Rhoda And Ted and All The Brilliant Minds Who Made The Mary Tyler Moore Show a Classic* digs deep into the whole Mary Tyler Moore universe, explained to this author in a 2017 interview that, to her way of thinking, there was no question about which came first, the women's movement or Mary Tyler Moore.

"The women's movement for sure," she said. "If anything, *The Mary Tyler Moore Show* was a little late…though it was probably more like right on time for mainstream culture, which is necessary for a television program to be successful."

Armstrong, who was a newborn when *The Mary*

Tyler Moore Show was entering its fifth season, and had played catch-up through extensive viewing and research over the ensuing years, now dodges the question of whether Moore was a feminist by accident or by design. "I think the whole question of Moore being a feminist might be pushing it here. She was certainly progressive in her own ways; and even when she became a feminist icon later with *The Mary Tyler Moore Show*, she didn't personally identify as such."

Differing opinions aside, it seemed like the perfect confluence of adding celebrity firepower to the growing women's movement. And it would be Steinem, whose *Ms. Magazine* had just published its premiere issue, who would offer Moore the opportunity to join the aggressive branch of the women's movement.

Moore listened to Steinem's invitation and, politely, turned it down.

"Gloria thought I was 100 percent on Betty Friedan's train and I really wasn't," she would repeatedly explain to Salon.com and countless other media outlets in the ensuing years. "I believed that women had a very major role to play as mothers. It's very necessary for mothers to be involved with their children and that's not what Gloria Steinem was saying. Gloria was saying that 'Oh you can have everything and you owe it to yourself to have a career.'

"And I didn't really believe in that."

Chapter One
Feeling Wild Anger

Nineteen thirty-six was a year to remember.

It was a leap year. And although World War II was still three years away, storm clouds and warning signs were in the air with the rise of Adolph Hitler and the saber rattling in Japan posting threatening headlines throughout the world. It was also the time of love, marriage and all the small moments that made up the lives of most people.

It was in the latter climate that Mary Tyler Moore was born on December 29, 1936 to George Tyler Moore and Marjorie Hackett Moore in Flatbush, Brooklyn. The Moore's came from good immigrant stock, George a mixture of English, Irish and German descent while Marjorie was a by-product of English immigrants. Given the WASP aesthetic of those pre-war years, Moore's parents were distinctive by their white-collar attitudes and influences. Her father was very well educated, a lover of classical music and classical literature. Her mother was an English major and a lover of the more artistic and theatrical pursuits.

Not surprising, both parents were well established Irish Catholics. And with the tenor of the times being what they were, George was the de facto breadwinner, working as a utilities company clerk, while Marjorie was quite content as the stay at home wife and mother.

Early on, Moore was a precocious and wildly observant little girl. Years later, in a conversation with *The Brooklyn Daily Eagle*, the actress recalled that her Brooklyn neighborhood was full of tree-lined front yards. "Some people had Fords or Hudsons. But everyone took the elevated train when they travelled to Manhattan to catch live shows or the latest movie and stage shows at Radio City Music Hall."

Moore gravitated toward the notion of theatrics as most young children did, indulging in childhood fantasy and taking every opportunity to be the center of attention. "I knew at a very early age what I wanted to do," she said in an *American Television* interview. "Some people refer to it as indulging in my instincts and artistic bent. I call it just showing off, which is what I did from about three years of age on."

Sadly, her parents would offer little in the way of emotional support or, for that matter, anything approaching a normal, loving home life. In a surprising bit of candor in a *USA Today* conversation, Moore disclosed "My parents thought that children should be born already 18, married and living in a neighboring town."

However, on occasion, Moore's parents would encourage her childhood fantasies. To outsiders, it might appear that her father, George, seemed present in his daughter's life but, in reality, he was not really of any significant emotional importance. "My father was very controlling and very remote," Moore told *Parade*.

Moore's candid assessment of her father did not stop there. Over the years she would not duck questions about the man who she seemed, by all accounts, to favor over her mother. And her honesty often stung with criticism. In a *Rolling Stone* article, she described her father as "a strict disciplinarian and not very affectionate." Even more hurtful was an excerpt from an early memoir *After All* which appeared in a *Washington Post* story when she matter-of -factly disclosed that "my father was bereft of the ability to express his love for me."

Being deprived of a true father/daughter relationship seemed something that the young Moore had put in a proper perspective and, at least publically, did not agonize over. When it came to her mother, a different set of realities had set in.

It seemed that the stresses of the marriage and the times (perhaps, even before the marriage) had driven Marjorie to alcoholism. During the pre-war years, alcoholism had not become a publically debated issue among families and was largely a private matter handled within the home, especially when it came to women. For Marjorie, the pain that led to drinking was palpable and made for a certain recklessness in the way she handled the issue.

Which in Moore's mother's case, was to largely ignore it. The reality was that while pregnant with Moore, Marjorie had continued to drink. The result was that, years later in her memoir *After All*, Moore described her 'off center and uneven facial features' as being the result of being the child of an alcoholic mother.' But growing up, Moore quickly became used to her mother's drinking as just part of her day-to-day life and, when feeling more charitable to her mother's plight, would dismiss it by saying "she was an entertaining alcoholic."

In a *National Public Radio* interview some years later, Moore would be somewhat more even handed and telling in the assessment of her parents. "My mother and father were very much the couple that Grant Tinker and I would become. WASP, repressed, unable to deal with things that are uncomfortable, pulling yourself up by their own bootstraps, not discussing anything that was truly ugly and unpleasant and just muddling through."

Parental dysfunction aside, Moore was growing up a seemingly normal child. No one could argue that she was well behaved and friendly. They lived in a tight knit blue-collar apartment complex and one of the family's closest friends, the Archers, lived right down the hall. But all of that changed when, at age six, Moore went to her mother with the news that Mr. Archer had molested her.

"I told my mother," Moore said in her autobiography *After All*, "I was six and so I was groping for words. The only word I knew for the entire genital area was wee wee for god's sake! My mother's response was 'No! That's not true!'

Moore would be downbeat and philosophical in addressing that moment in her memoir *After All*. "It's strange how events that change a life inside and out take no more than a moment."

Sadly, her mother's response was also not uncommon. At that time, child molestation by adults, often perpetrated by parents or close friends, was a subject that was usually pushed under the rug by the parents of the victims. It went down the road of dark, long held patriarchal values that men, quite simply, were prone to doing certain things and that their transgressions were often denied, even by the parents of the victims, for fear of being ostracized from their respective community and social circle. This was the attitude that Marjorie had, and most certainly believed, when her daughter had come to her. For the young girl, her mother's reaction cut deeply. "My mother, by her denial had abused me," Moore said in her autobiography. "My mother had abused me more than her friend."

But Moore was not about to let the matter pass unchallenged and, by the next day, the six-year-old had hatched a truly adult and diabolical way of getting even. "The next day I marched down the hall to the Archer's apartment. I was feeling wild anger. The family's son, six-year-old David Archer, answered. I told him exactly what his father had done to me. On his pale, small face, I saw the impact I had hoped for from my mother. I felt vindication and a little sick at what I had done to him."

But getting her revenge was quickly replaced by a sense of betrayal and disappointment directed toward her mother that, she admitted to *The Baltimore Sun*, would be with her forever. "I never felt the same about her again."

Chapter Two
Going to California

Moore's uncle would visit the family often during her childhood years.

It was a certainty that he saw the growing tensions and chaos within the family. Her father continued his unresponsive and unemotional ways and her mother had long since turned the corner into full blown alcoholism. For the young girl, it was a situation that she had long since grown to tolerate and it soon became an accepted part of her day-to-day life.

Another family milestone was the expansion of the Moore family. Her brother John's birth, some seven years later, was more a matter of expediency. Wartime regulations included an element that indicated that a man could not be drafted if he had a male offspring. Moore's parents brought John into the world, reportedly, to keep George out of the military. In that sense, they got lucky that their third child was a boy.

Moore's upbringing, not surprisingly, centered on a strict form of Catholicism as perpetuated by the nuns at St. Rose of Lima Parochial School. For Moore, her life was a stark contrast between home life and religious teachings. She was the prototypical good girl. But being that way had fostered a sense of defiance in the face of the forceful levels of religious obedience that were arbitrarily dished out by her parents and the nuns. Moore resented the numbing force of religion and had internally begun to be defiant in the face of it; testing, in subtle ways, the authority of religion in her life.

By the time Moore turned eight, her uncle's instincts about the young child had grown to a certainty.

Her uncle was an agent of the MCA/Universal entertainment corporation in Los Angeles and, as such, had a good idea of what went into a star in the making. In Moore's good nature, wide smile and a theatrical sense of her life, he saw potential and would always punctuate his visits to the Moore family with long stories and fabulous tales of the movie star life encouraging her parents to see that their daughter could have quite the career in Hollywood and that it was in their daughter's best interest that they move west.

Eventually Moore's parents agreed with the notion of their child as a star in Hollywood and the family, shortly after Moore turned nine in 1945, were on the road to Southern California. These were heady times in America. World War II had just come to a victorious conclusion and America was now transfused by a rebounding economic cycle. And the women's movement, still largely in its infancy, was steadily growing.

Although many decades removed from those earliest meetings at Seneca Falls, the women's movement began a gradual but earnest upturn during the late 40's and into the 50's. Reproductive rights for women was a hot topic, especially when the law of the land did an about face, declaring that sending information through the mail about birth control was no longer a federal crime. Women who worked in place of men in many positions during the war years were not so quick to want to return to the role of housewife and mother and the result was cries of equal employment and equal pay. Two of the earliest and most important feminist texts were published after the war, *The Second Sex (1949)* by Simone de Beauvoir and *The Feminine Mystique* by Betty Friedman (1963).

Moore's father immediately found work at the Southern California Gas Company and the family settled in to the American Dream in a post WWII cookie cutter neighborhood. But what Moore quickly found was that a change of locale did not necessarily translate into a change in her parents.

Moore's father continued to be as emotionally removed as ever and her mother continued to be the fun-loving alcoholic. "It was not the ideal home life," Moore tossed off in a *Los Angeles Times* interview.

In later years, Moore would diplomatically ascribe her growing estrangement from her parents largely to miscommunication, although to observers at the time it seemed that beneath the cheerful exterior there was a lot of resentment and no small amount of anger and sadness.

But Moore was easily distracted from her home life by her discovery of a new school, new friends and the flowering of her interest in dancing that resulted in the young girl taking her first formal dance lessons.

She would offer years later in a *Toronto Star* conversation that lessons were an emotional rollercoaster. Her first dance instruction was at the hands of a mentor/dance pianist from hell who would constantly scream at her to smile. Moore related that she was quite literally smiling out of terror and that, ultimately, that smile would, emotionally and physically, become attached to her face for the rest of her life.

Through her grade school and high school years (at Immaculate Heart High School), Moore, admittedly a very poor student, would focus primarily on dance, performing in countless recitals and gaining praise for her talent and promise for a certain professional Hollywood career. But eventually the contradiction of praise for her dancing ability and the emotional bleakness of her home life reached critical mass and, with the consent of Moore's parents, she left her home for the first of two prolonged absences, to live with her aunt and grandmother.

Moore had only fond memories of that time, especially of her Aunt Bertie who would ultimately supply the support and encouragement that was missing from her parents as she explained in *USA Today*. "Aunt Bertie sent me to dancing school, paid for the lessons, gave me singing lessons and told me I could do it. She encouraged me to always fight on and to get what I wanted."

Reports differ on the degree of separation that would last through her high school years. Some reports indicated she would only return to her parent's home on special occasions while others indicated that she would, sporadically, return to her parent's home to live for periods of time.

"Thank god I was not being abused in any way," she acknowledged to *The Ottawa Citizen* in discussing the reason she left home. "But I was seeking approval of some sort in many different ways."

As it turned out, her time away from her parents in the enthusiastic and supportive environment of her grandmother and aunt were just what Moore was searching for. They regularly attended her performances and always encouraged the young girl to try out for things and to get an agent. By the time Moore had turned 17, she had, indeed, acquired representation and, shortly after, her first professional job.

Moore was the pixie-like mascot Happy Hotpoint, the dancing elf who would prance in and out of commercials for The Hot Point Appliance Company, which aired during the reigning television series of the mid 50's, *The Adventures of Ozzie and Harriet.* Looking back on those commercials from the perspective of modern sensibilities can be, for many, an excruciating experience. Moore, dressed in a fuzzy-eared headpiece and a form-fitting leotard, was agonizing cheesy but largely a product of the way Hollywood operated in the 50's. Female characters with shapely bodies, broad smiles and nary a hint of character or personality were simply eye candy of the most blatant kind for the greater cause of selling kitchen appliances. But for her very first professional job, Moore found that it was easy work and, for the time, very lucrative.

The Happy Hotpoint shoot consisted of 39 commercial segments shot over the course of five days. Back in the day, that was considered good money for the time. The sponsors were quite happy and were all set to sign the now professional dancer up for a second round of Happy Hotpoint commercials.

There was only one slight glitch in their plans. By the time Moore turned 18 and was graduating from high school she was about to be married and would soon be noticeably pregnant. It was not an uncommon life change. Many teens go through a rebellious stage and ultimately see their escape from a restrictive lifestyle in early relationships and marriage. For Moore, her first taste of the Hollywood working world, slight as it was, may well have had something to do with it but, ultimately, it would be flight from a restrictive and unstable home life into what she considered the freedom and adventure of being a wife and mother.

In a late 70's interview with Barbara Walters, Moore admitted as much when she declared "I was going through a state, at about 16, 17, 18, where I didn't like my parents very much. I really wanted to be independent and I didn't want to be told what to do. There was this young man to whom I was obviously very attractive and I think I fell in love as much as you can fall in love at that age and I thought that it was right."

Moore thought of Richard Carleton Meeker as 'the boy next door.' He was in the sense that he lived in an apartment not far from the Moore family residence. But there was more to Meeker than good looks and availability.

At age 28, Meeker was a decade older than the young girl and, as a veteran of World War II and the Korean War, he was worldly in ways that Moore could barely comprehend. But it would be a safe bet that Moore was, secretly, looking for a daddy figure and, in a sense, the very security she seemed to be rebelling against. Which, as she would explain in her book *Growing Up Again: Life, Loves and Oh Yeah,*

Diabetes, was a big consideration in, after a whirlwind courtship, her accepting his marriage proposal.

"He had a job (a cranberry sauce sales manager) and his own apartment. So I accepted the invitation to get married on the condition that we moved at least four blocks away from my parents. For me, that was a real independent step."

Moore had met Meeker five months before she was due to graduate from Immaculate Heart High School. They would marry two months after graduation. Whirlwind courtships were not uncommon in post war America and, per society's traditional mores, were considered the next logical step for a woman with perceived few options. Moore put up a brave, defiant front in the face of her impending marriage but, truth be known, her next step was considered teenage rebellion more than outweighed by fear of the unknown.

Moore would often concede that she had taken small life steps in going from her parents' home to her husband's. "Living on my own was something that I had never done before," she told *Rolling Stone*. "I married right out of high school. I never really been on my own."

But she would put up a good front and proclaim to those around her that she was now truly on the road to adulthood and independence. And a big change would be her public parting of the ways with the Catholic religion. "I had a strong desire to lead my own life," she told *Rolling Stone*. "It was when I married that I broke formally with the Catholic Church which I had long considered a source of much guilt. I was determined to use birth control and that of course was a mortal sin. But I would end up pregnant two months after we were married. So much for my desire to stand on my own two feet."

Excited at the prospect of motherhood, Moore, nevertheless, continued to work in the guise of Happy Hotpoint and was well into a second round of commercials. Well into her third month of pregnancy, Moore insisted on keeping her secret from the network and, most importantly, the sponsors. While a woman getting pregnant was commonplace, in the stringent conservatism of Hollywood, an actress being with child and on camera was a lethal blow to the notion of women as sexual, fantasy beings. Moore sensed that the moment the Hotpoint people discovered her secret, she would be fired and, as she explained in a *Town & Country* magazine article, she took great pains to keep the sponsors guessing.

"Fitting into Happy's elf costume for the next block of commercials proved to be a challenge. I was now three months pregnant and my breasts reflected that fact. For a while I wore a special bra without cups to hide my secret. I was a bit egg-shaped but we got away with Happy's little secret for that group of ads. But finally the sponsors found out and the elf bit the dust and was replaced with another dancer. So off she, it, went. It was TV history."

Moore was disappointed as she had grown to love being in the spotlight. But the disappointment was more than salved by the notion that she was mere months away from being a mother. The remaining months went by in bliss. Richie was the attentive and loving husband and, reportedly, even her parents expressed a rare bit of positive feeling toward her.

Which may well have had a lot to do with the fact that Moore's parents were, coincidentally, pregnant with their third child. The Moore's third child, a girl named Elizabeth, was born within a couple of days of Moore going into labor and 19 years to the day that Moore was born.

Richie Meeker was born in Los Angeles on July 3, 1956. And, for a while, motherhood and fitting into a time honored societal mold was all that mattered as she would explain years later in her memoir *Growing Up Again: Life, Love and Oh Yeah Diabetes.*

"At the time I put meals on the table, cooed and rocked, cleaned and chatted with other moms in the park. I was cared for and I was the best mom I knew how to be."

Chapter Three
Second Spanish Girl

But within a year, Moore was getting restless. She loved being a mother and, by all accounts, was a very good one. However, Moore was starting to exhibit the restlessness of somebody who had just gotten into the realm of wife and mother without having experienced the rest of the world. By all accounts, Richie was patient with his wife, allowing that she would grow out of it and settle in to being a stay-at-home wife and mother.

Moore remained content with the domestic life until 1958. With her son now old enough to be left with more-than-willing family members for short periods, Moore stuck her toe back into the acting pool. What she found was that, despite a bit of publicity from her Happy Hotpoint commercials, the industry still looked upon her as a newcomer and, as such, the pickings were very slim.

And almost undetectable.

Technically, her first official film role was a 1958 comedy western entitled *Once Upon a Horse* that starred the rising comedy duo Rowan and Martin (who would go on to make television history some years later with their own comedy/variety show *Laugh In*). For her part, Moore's role was listed as 'dance hall girl.' Adding insult to injury, she was not credited. Her first television credit since the Happy Hotpoint days came in 1959 with a guest shot on an episode of *The George Burns Show*. She was listed as Mary Moore.

It would be the last time she would be known, professionally, as simply Mary Moore.

Turning 18 and almost immediately becoming a wife and mother was not an uncommon occurrence in the late 50's for women. But Moore felt, even as she fell into domesticity, that she had so much more to prove to the world. With no discernable skills other than dancing, many felt that she was not destined for much in life. But Moore was defiant in the face of those preconceptions.

"I was 18 years old and was determined to make my father proud and to prove to the sisters of Immaculate Heart High School that I would, indeed, amount to something," she would recall in accepting the Screen Actor's Guild Lifetime Achievement Award in 2012. And, in an excerpt from *The Dick Van Dyke Show Book*, she was even more assured. "I gave up college to become a star. I don't just hope for it. I work for it. I expect it."

Moore took her official professional step when she joined the Screen Actor's Guild. But when she found that there were six other Mary Moore's listed as members, she was advised to change her name so she would stand out from the crowd. "Change my name?" she recalled the incident at the SAG Lifetime Achievement Award presentation. "Come on! No! I'm Mary! Mary Moore! Everybody is going to know my name. Besides, what would my father say? It's his name too."

Then it hit her. Rather than change her name, she would simply include her middle name, Tyler, the name she shared with her dad. "I spoke it out loud," she related at the SAG awards. "Mary Tyler Moore sounded right. I wrote it down on my SAG registration form. It looked right."

That same year, Moore found sporadic work and continued anonymity as Student #1 in an episode of *Schlitz Playhouse* and would once again go uncredited in the role of 'Second Spanish Girl' in an episode of the television series *Steve Canyon.*

By the time Moore landed the role of the shadowy mystery secretary Sam in the series *Richard Diamond, Private Detective*, she was gaining in confidence even though she was far from getting rich. At her level, actor's guild money was topping out at $80 a week. And as she would quickly discover, nobody was willing to let on that there was an actual flesh and blood actress attached to the role. Over the course of the first eight episodes, Moore either went as 'uncredited,' 'voice' or 'secretary,' most likely in line with the show trying to play up the mystery angle on a show that, in all honesty, was pretty much a cookie cutter private eye and bad guys series.

Finally Moore had had enough. She went to the show's producers and demanded a pay raise in lieu of the lack of publicity. Her demand would be met with termination after her then-current contract would end in five episodes. But Moore, in a totally uncharacteristic move by a woman, let alone an actress for the time, would refuse to go quietly into that good night. In a totally canny, and yes risky move, Moore launched her own publicity blitz, telling anyone who would listen that Mary Tyler Moore was the actual face and body of Sam. The result would be a mountain of press that would appear during the run of her last appearances on *Richard Diamond* that effectively put her on the Hollywood radar and had casting agents all over town falling all over themselves to cast her.

Consequently, the day she left the *Richard Diamond, Private Detective* soundstage for the last time, she, suddenly in the hands of a topflight agent, literally walked into the arms of just about every show in town. The early 60's were a highwater mark for television. Lots of shows were being turned out on the big three networks with as many as 25-30 episodes a season. There was a lot of work to go around and, between 1959-61 for the right type, and Moore was suddenly that type.

Although still a relative newcomer to the way Hollywood worked, Moore quickly learned one important element to how show business worked. Rule number one being don't say no to anything until you are in a position to say no.

And even when there were no acting roles available, the ever-resilient Moore always seemed to manage a paycheck. Her dancing ability came in handy when she managed a recurring role in the chorus lines, of *The Eddie Fisher Show,* a comedy/music/variety show, and similar shows fronted by Jimmy Durante, George Gobel, Dean Martin and Jerry Lewis. Her physical beauty, and in particular, her trademark shapely legs, also made her the darling of a recording cycle in which producers would churn out schmaltzy music of the day with session musicians and found Moore's seductive (for the time) look as ideal album cover fodder. Moore would do more than a dozen of these, admittedly, cheesy album photo-shoots, with such cornball titles as *Cha Cha Cha*, *Organ Favorites*, *Dance to the Latin Beat* and *The Roaring 20's*, which, in later years, would become quite the novelty/collectable.

Among the early 60's shows that Moore would appear in were *Johnny Staccato, Bachelor Father*, *Overland Trail*, *The Tab Hunter Show*, *Bourbon Street Beat*, *77 Sunset Strip*, *Surfside Six*, *Wanted Dead or Alive* and *Hawaiian Eye*. It was during this period that Moore made her first, high on the cast list, appearance in a movie in *X-15* opposite another star in the making, Charles Bronson. Moore was alternately amazed and bemused at the sudden burst of activity in an excerpt from *The Dick Van Dyke Show Book* when she offered "Other shows just seemed to want to use the girl who played Sam."

But the sudden notoriety seemed to have the desired effect. Moore was now going up for progressively more and more substantial parts. One in particular would ultimately prove to be a pivotal turning point. *The Danny Thomas Show* aka *Make Room For Daddy*, a comedy series that found Thomas as a night club performer also dealing with the foibles and pit falls of everyday family life. The role Moore went up for was that of Thomas' older daughter. Moore and Thomas hit it off immediately during her audition and, on the surface, it appeared that she had a real shot at landing her first on-screen recurring series role.

But as it turned out, all the talent in the world was not going to overcome one insurmountable problem. The actress had a button nose. And, if you've ever seen a picture of Thomas, his nose was anything but.

"She missed it by a nose," legendary producer/director/writer Carl Reiner said in the book *My Lucky Life in and Out of Show Business*. In the same book, Thomas was more succinct. "No daughter of mine could ever had a nose that small."

However Moore was persistent. When told the reason why she did not get the part, she reportedly told Thomas that she would get a bump surgically added to her nose if that would get her the part. Thomas laughed at the half serious offer.

But she still did not get the part.

Chapter Four
Oh Rob!

With the onset of 1961, Moore was suddenly a professionally sound, working actress. It seemed at times that she had more work at any one moment than she could handle. Personally, her life was on the rocks.

Moore had remained steadfast in wanting to lead her own life and make it in Hollywood. Consequently, she was spending more time working and less time being the at-home wife and mother that had seemed so wonderful in the beginning and had progressively spiraled down into an afterthought. Meeker and Moore had become strangers and as her career began to blossom, their marriage crumbled.

But the real tragedy, as Moore would explain in her autobiography *Growing Up Again: Life, Loves and Oh Yeah Diabetes*, was that she was feeling guilt over being, to her way of thinking, a bad mother. "Truth be told, work was my main focus before, during and after (we had their child). If I had it to do over again, I wouldn't have pursued a career if I had a little boy to take care of."

Which was why Moore was not in a good place, mentally and emotionally, two weeks into the New

Year when she was called in to audition for something called *The Dick Van Dyke Show*. It the brainchild of Carl Reiner who was attempting to channel his real life work on the classic series *Your Show of Shows* into a comedy romp chronicling the personal and professional life of a television writer and his wacky friends and family. One of the starring roles, that of the writer's wife, Laura Petrie, a dancer who gave up the life to be a supportive and often comically frustrated housewife to her husband, seemed tailor-made for Moore and Reiner requested that she come in for an audition,

Moore and her husband were in the process of finalizing what would become a legal separation and, as Reiner would recall in the book *The Dick Van Dyke Show Book*, professionally it had been a rough week. "She had already been on three or four auditions that week and they had not gone well. And we call and she's decided not to go on another one. Her feeling was that 'That's it! I'm out of this! I'm never going on another audition.'

"But at the last minute, she decided to go."

By the time Moore had agreed to go to the audition, *The Dick Van Dyke Show* was already the subject of no small amount of intrigue. An earlier incarnation of the show, entitled *Head of the Family* featuring a largely different cast, had been shot and ultimately rejected. When it came time for the reshoot, the hotly contested title role of Rob Petrie had boiled down to two actors, Dick Van Dyke and Johnny Carson. It was Van Dyke's Broadway reputation in *Bye Bye Birdie* that ultimately swayed the decision in his favor.

None of that was of any concern to Moore as she went in for the audition. The only thing on her mind was fear of the genius she perceived as Reiner. "I was so nervous when I went in to read for him," she recalled in *The Dick Van Dyke Show Book*. "I did not realize I was going to actually be reading for him and almost blew it because of my awe for him as a performer."

In the same book, Reiner would relate that her audition was nothing short of miraculous. "She walked into the office, sat down and she read the first three lines of the pilot script. That's all it took, three lines. And I heard the sound. She said hello like a real person."

Reiner put his hand lovingly on the top of the amazed actress and marched her down to the office of the show's executive producer, Sheldon Leonard, where he proceeded to praise her to the skies. Leonard took a not overly interested look at the nervous Moore and said okay. Just like that, Moore was now the co-star of what would hopefully be a hit series with a long run. There was only one final hurdle to her getting the job. She had to convince her co-star Van Dyke. And that was not going to be easy.

At age 35, the actor was well versed in how societal mores' influenced much of popular culture of the day. And he was very concerned that the ten-year difference between the two actors would impact the perception of viewers with conservative values. He expressed his concern to both Leonard and Reiner in *The Dick Van Dyke Show Book*.

"I just thought God Almighty! This is never going to work. Mary's too young for me."

Reiner and Van Dyke initially agreed to disagree. It also did not help that the actor's agent was not thrilled with the premise of the show and was encouraging his client to drop out of the project. But Reiner, ever the creative despot, came up with an outlandish solution. "I told them both I want you to go away and spend the weekend together. Given the already shaky status of her marriage, Moore blanched at the prospect. But Van Dyke got the point Reiner was trying to make. "We didn't take him up on his offer but he was making the point that if you don't really like each other, no amount of good acting or writing is gonna make people think you do."

Van Dyke and Moore agreed to give it a try and, as they prepped for the upcoming pilot shoot, they found the chemistry in character and as people. The bottom line was that they truly did like each other.

On the surface, *The Dick Van Dyke Show* was being chatted up primarily in the industry. Moore's sudden ascension from total unknown to co-starring in a series that many were holding out high hopes for was good for some fan magazine coverage. But, in hindsight, the show, even with its stellar pedigree behind the scenes and with its largely veteran cast, was basically more of the same sitcom format that had settled into the television industry as a tool of conservative and middle American sponsors who, whether anybody wanted to admit it or not, were the deciding voice on what made it to the airwaves.

The finished product would be, by modern day sensibilities, almost laughingly sexist. Laura was the cliché wife and mother who dared not think in terms of a career and a life outside the home. If she did, she was immediately labeled as wrong and her long-suffering, hard- working husband was always right. Nobody in the television universe was ready, willing or able to fight that notion. At least not in the obvious ways

The Dick Van Dyke Show predated modern feminism and, truth be known, if you take away the fact that the character of Sally Rogers (played by Rose Marie) was single and the aforementioned pants vs dresses controversy would be all the rage, it was all pretty pat, perhaps with a little more spunk than a lot of what was being offered at the time, but still fairly status quo.

It was a stretch to say that *The Dick Van Dyke Show* was ahead of its time in dealing with feminist issues in anything approaching a progressive manner. The best author Armstrong could summon up was "to some extent, yes."

Consequently, as Moore, Van Dyke and the rest of the cast began to prepare for the pilot episode, there were already signs that progress would be slow in coming. One of the most glaring and laughable examples of this was that the Petrie bedroom continued to have two separate beds. But, perhaps of even more importance, was that certain words continued to remain taboo…

…The most jarring being the word "pregnant" which, according to the unofficial bible of *The Dick Van Dyke Show*, was a definite no no, as was even the hint, in action or deed, that a television couple was actually having sex. Which, after more than a dozen stereotypical guest shots on late 50's/early 60's network television, did not come as a surprise to

Moore shortly after receiving the character breakdown of Laura as she would recall in a *National Public Radio* interview.

“Laura was going to be a wife, a television wife and that really had its classical parameters and dimensions that were established and hardly ever varied. If the wife was the star of the show, she was the funny one. But all the television wives were kind of obedient.”

Chapter Five
Car Crash Love

Moore's separation and impending divorce, coupled with the activity and hoopla surrounding her break-through television role did not leave the actress much time to contemplate the notion that she was suddenly single again. But she was well aware that she was about to once again enter a certain stage in life albeit little bit late.

"I had never really lived a kind of single life," she told *National Public Radio*. But mere weeks into once again being on her own, the actress was suddenly smitten. As was the custom, important people in the industry were often allowed to observe the earliest stages of a new TV series. Such was the case in mid-January 1961 when a young advertising executive named Grant Tinker was invited by producer Sheldon Leonard to observe a run through of the pilot episode of *The Dick Van Dyke Show*.

Tinker and Moore were casually introduced on the set. It did not appear that there were any sparks. But one thing was certain, Tinker was suddenly finding any excuse to fly out to Los Angeles on business and, by association, to ingratiate himself into

The Dick Van Dyke Show social circle. There always seemed to be good-natured banter between Tinker and Moore and, in a friendly sort of way, they always seemed to be together.

But Tinker was a man of character and principal. He was well aware that Moore was just coming out of a marriage and, although there was a sense that the pair had become mutually smitten with each other, he refused to ask her out on a real date until she was officially divorced. But as it turned out, the pair's growing feelings for each other did allow for mild amusement and speculation among *The Dick Van Dyke Show* family.

At the conclusion of one after-show get together, Associate Producer Ron Jacobs recalled in *The Dick Van Dyke Show Book* that Moore was leaving the party in her car. A few moments later Tinker followed in his car. Moments later Jacobs and other party-goers were startled by a loud crash coming from down the street. "We all laughed," said Jacobs. "We all said 'Grant must have run into Mary.' It was meant as a joke but then we looked down the street and into traffic. Mary had stopped suddenly and Grant had ploughed right into the back of her car."

Eventually Moore's divorce was final and, during an October 1961 promotional tour in New York, Moore and Tinker went out on their first official date. By all first date standards, it seemed fairly low-key as the couple took in the Broadway show *Mary, Mary* and then danced the night away at New York's trendy Peppermint Lounge. The consensus from those privy to the specifics of the date was that Tinker was a perfect gentleman. As for Moore…

…"I woke up the next morning," she told *TV Guide*, "and I knew I was in love."

But nobody else seemed to know. For the next nine months, Tinker and Moore's relationship was so low-key and clandestine that nobody in their respective inner circles had a clue that they were even in a relationship, let alone romantically involved. That they would get together socially and make time for each other on either coast was just considered part and parcel of the Hollywood lifestyle and social scene. On the surface, both had budding careers that seemingly consumed their waking hours. But the reality was that they had grown quickly in love and had deepened their relationship was the celebrity world's best kept secret well into 1962.

When, six months after the end of Moore's first marriage, it became huge Hollywood news that Tinker and she would be tying the knot on June 1, 1962.

Chapter Six
Something in the Air

It was a big year for the women's rights movement.

In 1960, The Food And Drug Administration approved the oral contraceptive pill and, by 1961, the 'pill' was readily available to the public. That same year, President John F. Kennedy's Presidential Commission On the Status of Women reported to the world that rampant discrimination existed in every aspect of American life and, subsequently, put forth extensive proposals to achieve equality that included fair housing practices, paid maternity leave and affordable childcare.

On October 3, 1961, *The Dick Van Dyke Show* was making its television premiere and, behind the scenes show creator Carl Reiner was doing his best, with Moore's participation, to steer the portrayal of women in television in a more progressive direction. Make no mistake, the show's feminist sense was subtle and elusive, relying, especially in the case of the character Laura, on optimism and good-natured innocence rather than any sense of rebellion and flag waving. In essence, the relationship between Rob and Laura was a day-to-day walk in the real world with conflicts, laughs and happy endings. The show was not that much different than a number of shows that had come before. Except, as one observer deftly put it, their day-to-day lives were much deeper than what was going on with their kid that day.

It was an experimental show that was inching toward a new way of thinking and, in Moore, Reiner had found the ideal conduit for the tiny steps forward. At a very young age, Moore was possessed of an innate sense of style, comedy and an uncanny ability to latch onto the character of Laura and make her her own in an experienced, real world way that belayed the actress's young age.

Moore realized that the role of Laura would not just be another cookie-cutter housewife. The prospect played on her fears and insecurities but ultimately drove her to the challenge as she offered in her memoir *After All*. "I have always chosen work that challenges me because if I don't go into work a little scared, I don't have any interest in it."

And once Moore put her foot down and brought the whole vacuuming in a dress and high heels to a halt, there was the question of sex. The bedroom decorum, with its two separate beds, was in the see-no-evil, hear-no-evil, say-no-evil tradition of a long sponsor-driven of history of chastity on the small screen. With the emerging daring of Reiner, and the believable chemistry and banter of Rob and Laura, it was evident from the get-go that yes they were having sex, probably lots of it and in a quite normal familial way.

"Rob and Laura were a modern couple," Van Dyke told *CBS News*. "You know that these people have sex."

Years later, Van Dyke would tell *The Hollywood Reporter* that in the roll up to that first season, there was some concern of how Moore's comedic chops would hold up against such seasoned jokesters as himself, Morey Amsterdam and Rose Marie. Apparently, there was little to fear. "I don't know what made her comic timing so great. Mary just picked it up so fast. She had us all laughing after a couple of episodes. She just grabbed onto the character."

And it was to the show's writer's credit that *The Dick Van Dyke Show* did not waste any time incorporating Moore's talents into the series. In the first season's second episode, entitled "My Blonde Haired Brunette," in which Laura, feeling that the spark has gone out of their marriage, decides that becoming a blonde might spice things up. Moore played the scenario spot on, alternately laugh inducing and sympathetic, until the end when Laura's blonde attempt has resulted in Moore bursting into tears of frustration and embarrassment with her head now in a monstrous black and white cookie look. It was a simple premise that, in Moore's hands, added real world pathos to the comedy.

In a conversation with *Entertainment Weekly*, Moore offered that this particular episode was a pivotal moment for her career. "I bleached my hair blond and only got half of it dyed back. I got to cry for the first time. That opened everybody's eyes up to the fact that I could do some funny stuff."

Another first season standout, and what many consider the best episode of the inaugural season was "The Curious Thing About Women" whose storyline centered around Rob deciding to write a sketch based on Laura's penchant for opening his mail. It was the perfect balance of office and home life but the big laughs would come in Moore's tour de force slapstick routine centered around her temptations and the consequences of proving Rob wrong.

By the time the first season came to an end, creatively the show had found the perfect balance between Van Dyke and Moore and had gained critical praise for the progressive way in which the writers had created an equal in Laura rather than a stereotypical subordinate. Unfortunately, the ratings were not very good. The show had been up against the wildly popular *The Perry Como Show* and despite giving the show a full airing of its 16 episode first season, *The Dick Van Dyke Show* was languishing at No. 80 in the national ratings and the network was strongly considering canceling *The Dick Van Dyke Show*, largely because advertiser Proctor & Gamble who were already making waves by objecting to Moore wearing Capri pants instead of a dress and high heels, were strongly considering pulling their advertisement from the show.

What ultimately saved *The Dick Van Dyke Show* from ratings oblivion depends on which story you believed. *The Dick Van Dyke Show Book* floated the story that Proctor & Gamble were in actuality so enamored of the show that they threatened to pull all their advertising off the CBS daytime shows if the network did not keep the show on the air. Another tale postulated by *The New York Post* and others had Carl Reiner and producer Sheldon Leonard going to Proctor & Gamble headquarters to convince them to save the show. P&G reportedly agreed to fund half the show while Kent Cigarettes was poised to advertise the other half. Eventually Proctor & Gamble agreed to give *The Dick Van Dyke Show* its full financial blessing. Given the reprieve, CBS went all in on saving the show, slotting it on the same night as their mammoth hit *The Beverly Hillbillies*. Not surprisingly, the ratings went through the roof and *The Dick Van Dyke Show* flourished during the next four years of its five-year run.

For Moore, the next four years would be a mixed bag. The show quickly evolved into an Emmy Award perennial. Moore's talent was almost immediately recognized as well. For the 1962-63 season, the actress was nominated for the Outstanding Continued Performance By An Actress In A Series. It was an award she would capture in the succeeding two seasons. On the occasion of her first Emmy, she enthusiastically told *ABC News* "I know this will never happen again."

But the pressures of stardom would eventually take their toll. During the run of the show, the pressures of being in the eye of Hollywood would drive Van Dyke to drinking which led to full-blown alcoholism and eventually rehab. For Moore, the grind of making a weekly television series, likewise, began to show itself, albeit in less obvious ways. The actress began to experience occasional dizziness, noticeable weight loss and bouts of blurred vision. She chalked it up to being overworked and went on about her business and ignored the warning signs that, some years later, would later be diagnosed…

…As Type 1 Diabetes.

More pressing at the time was the guilt of being a

failure at motherhood at a time when the burgeoning women's movement was preaching that it was all right for women to have it all. In her autobiography *After All*, Moore acknowledged the guilt. "By the time Ritchie was five, I had already let him down. When he needed me the most, I was busier and more self-concerned."

On one level, Moore was seemingly living the feminist dream. But as she would later reflect in her memoir *Growing Up Again: Life, Loves and Oh Yeah Diabetes*, Moore was candid in admitting that, despite her best efforts, she was, in fact, coming up short when it came to balancing career and motherhood. "When the marriage ended, I landed the role on *The Dick Van Dyke Show* and I proudly realized that I could take care of Ritchie and myself, at least economically. But, emotionally, I was not ready to take the helm.

"My heart breaks when I think of the times I missed."

Chapter Seven
Can You Beat This?

The last episode of *The Dick Van Dyke Show* had barely faded out in 1966. But Moore was already looking forward to bigger and better things. And those better things loomed large on the big screen.

Creatively speaking, the mid-60's were a time of daring. Concepts and challenging stories were everywhere in the minds of an emerging younger generation inside the film industry. *Bonnie and Clyde*, *The Graduate* and *In The Heat of The Night* immediately jumped to the level of classic cinematic art in their frank depiction of sex, violence and social and political mores. The ultimate flight of fancy *2001: A Space Odyssey*, the harsh reality of *Midnight Cowboy* and the anti-establishment battle cry of *Easy Rider* were waiting in the wings.

Compared to these and others, the work Moore had done to that point appeared quaint and dated. But the reality was that Moore would have been quite content to continue *The Dick Van Dyke Show* for another couple of seasons. The intimacy of doing television was a perfect fit for her talents and sensibilities. She had loved the family nature of the production and, in the best possible way, it was sealed off from the real world. But when Van Dyke and Reiner decided enough was enough, Moore took a next bold step and an unexpected one at that. She was Broadway bound in a much-anticipated adaptation of *Breakfast at Tiffany's*.

The cast, which would also include Richard Chamberlin and Sally Kellerman, and was based on the 1961 Truman Capote novella. Directed by Abe Burrows and produced by David Merrick, *Breakfast at Tiffany's* seemed a natural next step for Moore. But during a protracted out of town series of shows in preparation for its official Broadway premiere, it soon became evident that the entire production was in over its collective head.

There were constant problems in the script and musical score. The director quit when a rewrite was ordered by producer Merrick, new script pages were given to the actors on a daily basis, mere hours before a performance, and the overall production had ballooned to an unwieldy four hours. Needless to say, morale was low among the cast, most notably with Moore whose inconsistency on a large theatrical stage was palpable. At one point, Moore was convinced that producer Merrick was going to fire her shortly after the musical's official unveiling.

Breakfast at Tiffany's limped to Broadway late in December 1966 on the wings of massive pre-sale ticket sales and anticipation. The show ran four performances before producer Merrick closed it down. The press was diplomatic in chronicling the premature demise of the play. There seemed enough blame to go around. But the not too-veiled intimations that the problems lay specifically at the feet of Moore cut the deepest.

Moore took the closure hard. It was an emotional and ego driven attack on her long-held beliefs as she offered to *The New York Daily News*. "I was brought up to believe in happy endings. If you prayed for something long enough you got it." Consequently, the premature failure of *Breakfast at Tiffany's* really hurt. "I did take it absolutely on my shoulders for a long time," Moore told the *Daily News*. "Nobody else felt it was my fault but I had my tail very much between my legs."

The long held Studio System, which allowed studios to put actors with star promise under a contract that would allow them to dictate which films they appeared in, had been the topic of some controversy for decades as more and more big name actors successfully fought for their freedom. By the mid-60's the Studio System was largely on the decline. Moore may well have been one of the last actors of note to go into such an agreement when she signed an exclusive contract with Universal Pictures. Moore, most likely, felt the overall quality of Universal films would put her in line for advancing her career. But, according to a blog by actor/comedian Eddie Deezen in Neatorama.com, Universal had other ideas.

Legendary actress Doris Day was winding down her film career, starring in an admittedly slight comedy called *With Six You Get Eggroll* and Universal, behind closed doors, was looking to Moore as a likely candidate to inherit Day's mantle of 'America's Sweetheart.' But Moore's first film under the Universal agreement would be light years removed from that notion.

Thoroughly Modern Millie was a star studded, big budget movie musical of the old school. It was light-hearted, alternately comedic and charming and, in a positive, entertaining way, as predictable and familiar right down to the proverbial happy ending.

Moore's dancing and better than expected singing talents made her the ideal charmer, Dorothy Brown who comes to New York in 1922 with the goal of working for and marrying a rich man. Along the way she falls in with some like-minded women who overcome all obstacles en route to getting their hearts' desire.

Thoroughly Modern Millie opened in 1967 at the height of the so-called reemergence of a second wave of feminism and was totally contrary to what was going on in the ever-advancing women's movement. The film was a box office smash and, if the reviews were any indication, Universal had found their leading lady primed and ready for light hearted fare.

Moore would have her comedic talents tested the following year with co-starring roles in two very slight and largely forgotten comedies, *Don't Just Stand There*, an on the cheap sex comedy opposite Robert Wagner and Moore in a brunette wig, and *What's So Bad About Feeling Good?*, with George Peppard in a comedy with science fiction overtones about a virus that infects people with happiness. The latter film did okay box office, the former next to nothing which, in turn, left Moore and Universal in a bit of a quandary. These were not the kinds of films that would establish Moore in anything resembling a wholesome character. Moore was getting restless at her seeming lack of progress and Universal was rapidly running out the string on options.

Rather than attempting to shoehorn Moore into another B movie with other up and coming performers, Universal tried something different. *Change of Habit* would be created totally for Moore to star in and, in inception, would create a transition for Moore into the next generation's Doris Day.

Change of Habit offered up the tale of three nuns who go undercover to try and help out in an inner city ghetto. Along the way they meet another ghetto volunteer, a doctor who strikes emotional and romantic sparks with Moore's character as she contemplates giving up her religious vows to follow her heart. On the surface *Change of Habit* read as a serviceable romantic drama with commercial potential and, most importantly, a break-out role for Moore.

But all of that suddenly changed when Elvis Presley was cast as the male lead.

What had originally been a Mary Tyler Moore vehicle quickly transformed into yet another Elvis film with typical Elvis musical moments shoehorned into the script. But what must have galled Moore no end was that Elvis's name was now at the top of the cast list and all the promotion. Which, truth be known, was not the singer's idea. Elvis movies had long since hit the downward slide of formula, mediocrity and predictability. They continued to make money but, as witness his previous attempt at a serious acting role in *Charro*, the profits were rapidly diminishing.

Moore recalled in a Neatorama.com article that Elvis was after recognition as a legitimate actor. "He was looking for a film that would require none of the rock star gyrations, but would illuminate his acting ability. Apparently, the studio (Universal) was able to convince Elvis that the choice would pave the way for dramatic recognition."

By the time *Change Of Habit* began filming, Moore had more important things than Elvis's film career to deal with. The early symptoms exhibited during the filming of *The Dick Van Dyke Show* were progressing and, although it would be 1970 before Moore would be officially diagnosed with Type 1 Diabetes, the symptoms had progressed to the point where she became withdrawn and not very sociable with the rest of the *Change of Habit* cast and crew. Co-star Jane Elliott was quoted in Neatorama.com as recalling, "She didn't get involved. She didn't socialize." In the same article, co-star Barbara McNair related, "I didn't talk to her much because she was kind of stand-offish. She wasn't easy to get to know. She didn't socialize, so I never got to know her."

Moore would typically eat her meals alone in her dressing room. It was speculated that the main reason for her not eating with the cast and crew had been, with the prognosis of Type 1 Diabetes, doctors had already proscribed a special diet and that she did not want to appear self-conscious or answer questions. Virginia Vincent, a *Change of Habit* actress, told Neatorama that she once saw Moore eating an apple during a lunch break and asked her, "All you're eating for lunch is an apple?" To wit Moore replied, "Yes, that's it."

Although Moore was still quite young, the onset of Diabetes had the effect of causing her skin to prematurely wrinkle. To offset this problem, the director of photography Russ Metty would resort to using a special light on Moore when filming her scenes that would disguise the wrinkles with a glowing effect.

Elvis would often brag that he had slept with every one of his leading ladies except one. Years later Moore would relate in a *Parade Magazine* interview she acknowledged that of all the leading men she had worked with, Elvis was more her type. "I think it was Elvis because he went so against the grain." In hindsight, an on-set romance between the two co- stars seemed inevitable. But while the pair did a cautious dance during the filming of *Change of Habit*, ultimately it never evolved beyond the mild flirtation stage.

For her part, Moore had developed a highly advanced sense when it came to men. She instinctively knew when they were interested in her and she was flattered by the attention. But seeing as how they were both married at the time and had children, Moore, in her own way, put a halt to anything beyond mild flirtation.

"He confessed right from the start that he had a crush on me from *The Dick Van Dyke Show,*" she said in the Neatorama piece. "He was so shy about it, he was literally kicking at the dirt below him as we talked. He had a tendency to call me 'ma'am' out of respect even though I was younger than him. It was a wonderful experience. He was charming and he had a big crush on me, almost like a young kid with an older woman. He was shy."

Universal had high hopes in the days leading up to the November, 1969 release of *Change of Habit*. Sadly, it would not be the box office smash everybody was hoping for. The reviews were decidedly mixed and although the movie did make back its cost, beyond that the profits were slim. For both stars the disappointment was evident. It would be Elvis' last attempt at a real acting career. Moore saw the movie as another knock against her making the transition from television star to movie star.

Those post *Dick Van Dyke Show* film choices were seen as fluff rather than strong message pictures. But author Armstrong, in an interview with the author only marginally agreed. "*Thoroughly Modern Millie* was about women on their own in the big city which is kind of progressive in tone and *Change of Habit* was about her character, a nun, helping out in a needy city neighborhood. But those are also probably more reflections of the times than reflections on her personally."

Contrary to the sudden stagnation of her career and the spiraling downward of any perceived star power, the real world, especially the second wave of the feminist movement, was chugging along at a brisk pace. The women's movement had become increasingly demonstrative and forthright in making demands. The same year *Change of Habit* was dying a box office death, members of the radical feminist group, The Redstockings, were making headlines when they stormed into a New York legislature hearing on abortion laws, chaired by 14 white men and a nun, demanding that all anti-abortion laws be repealed. It was the same year that the first incarnation of the influential Pro-Choice America group was founded.

For her part, Moore was quietly dealing with her lack of success but, as an afterthought, Moore did one more movie on her Universal contract, a very atmospheric/murder mystery opposite international star Louis Jordan entitled *Run a Crooked Mile*. The film, despite good reviews with many citing Moore's portrayal as easily one of the best of her career, was in and out of theaters with nary an acknowledgement of its existence.

That Moore received good reviews in it was of little consolation. Professionally, Moore was down in the dumps.

Chapter Eight
The Other Woman

In spite of all the good reviews in her post-*Dick Van Dyke Show* career, casting directors could not be persuaded away from the indelible stereotype of Moore as wife, mother and the person that served people coffee.

In the worst possible Hollywood nightmare, Moore was being dismissed and hopelessly stereotyped while her obvious talents were being ignored. *Change of Habit* would also be a literal shock to Moore's psyche. She was so visibly shaken at the prospect of doing another movie and, in fact, it would be another 11 years before Moore would even consider another studio film. She was mentally backed into a corner with no clear way out.

Author Armstrong conceded that Moore had several reasons for feeling down and out. "She certainly was at a career low point. I don't know how she was feeling and I don't know if she was thinking about giving up acting. But a lot of bad stuff had just happened. Her movie career was stalled, her star turn on Broadway in the musical *Breakfast at Tiffany's* notoriously bombed, she had miscarried and she was diagnosed with diabetes. So one can guess that she wasn't feeling great."

So much so that she agreed to take a career step backwards when, sometime after filming *Change of Habit*, she appeared in a Pepsodent toothpaste commercial that came and went rather quickly and, to this day, remains little seen and little remembered. Which, to Moore's way of thinking, was just fine with her.

Personally, things were not going much better. The strained relationship between her son Ritchie and herself were adding to Moore's unhappiness. She had been hoping that Tinker would help the relationship by stepping in as Ritchie's surrogate father but would ultimately be disappointed. "I was hoping that Grant would be a father figure for Ritchie," she told *The Washington Post*. "Grant had the same expectations of children that he had for himself, leaving little room for failure. Ritchie was almost always falling short."

Adding to her misery was that, unbeknownst to most in her circle, Tinker and Moore were attempting to have a child of their own. Things seemed to be going well until sometime after the release of *Change of Habit* when Moore miscarried. Sadness would be balanced out by a silver lining when, in the immediate aftermath of the miscarriage, a routine blood test produced the diagnosis that Moore, after months of speculation, did, indeed, have Type 1 Diabetes. "Moore recalled in *The Washington Post* that "Normal blood sugar levels are somewhere between 70 and 110. Mine was 750 and the doctors were amazed that I was still walking around."

A ray of sunshine in Moore's dark period would

emerge in the guise of old friend Dick Van Dyke who appeared out of nowhere with an offer that would lift her spirits.

News of any kind travels fast in Hollywood and, in regards to Moore's recent lack of success, it was a safe bet that Van Dyke knew and, perhaps in his own way, was looking to help his partner out. Using his clout, Van Dyke recalled in a *Vanity Fair* conversation that "We hooked up this special called *Dick Van Dyke and The Other Woman* with the idea of showing off everything she could do.

Moore was thrilled when Van Dyke called with his plan. "Dick called and said 'I'm going to do a special called *Dick Van Dyke and The Other Woman*. The other woman would be you because every time I try to check into a hotel with my wife, they look at me as though I'm cheating on Laura.' "

On paper, *Dick Van Dyke and The Other Woman* seemed tailor made for Moore. It was largely a musical outing that would play right into her song and dance skills. The comedy elements were very television/very Dick Van Dyke Show. It would be on her old flagship station CBS so it would give her lots of exposure.

Moore did not have to think about it. She said yes immediately.

The reality was that, by Hollywood standards, she had very few options. Her perceived failures on the big screen made small parts in future projects her only option. She was still young enough that she could return to dancing full time but that was a hit or miss proposition that would, most likely, not guarantee notoriety. In her darkest moments, Moore may well have considered getting out of the business altogether and being the supportive spouse to Tinker. But when Van Dyke came calling, Moore saw the opportunity to return to her strengths which lay in television.

Not surprisingly, *Dick Van Dyke and The Other Woman* had a very down home, nostalgic feel to it as Moore and Van Dyke revisited their fictional relationship between Rob and Laura through a series of sketches and song and dance numbers that probed the ins and outs of the fictional, television sitcom life as well as aspects of Laura that allowed Moore full reign to showcase her talents.

The ease and comfort with which Moore was able to return to that old television/Dick Van Dyke vibe was evident. A dance number centered around skiers on crutches was a rolling in the aisles, extremely well-choreographed bit of old school shtick that still seemed to work. On a more sentimental level, Moore and Van Dyke's take as wedding cake figures was solid in its interpretation of both real and fictional life. It was all very family friendly and geared toward those who had followed Laura in the *The Dick Van Dyke Show*. If anything was out there and evenly remotely feminist in the show, it was Moore in an enticing solo song and dance segment that paid homage to the concept of the American Woman. In it, Moore incorporated the iconic images of flappers, suffragettes, and the iconic image of Rosie the Riveter as well as the modern woman (in the 60's). Moore appeared quite confident in what many considered a show-stopping moment where the viewers sensed that Moore was totally at home on the small screen and that any future projects would, most likely, be in that arena.

The reviews for *Dick Van Dyke and The Other Women* were overwhelmingly positive and the ratings immediately bore that out. CBS was thrilled, so much so that the network immediately offered both Van Dyke and Moore separate pilot deals that would allow them to do any kind of half hour show they wanted. It was an unheard of offer.

And Moore was ready and willing to take advantage of it. But not at first.

Chapter Nine

Divorce is All Around

Moore was thrilled at the prospect but still feeling insecure.

The idea of starring in a series that would appeal, per CBS's edict, to a more sophisticated audience that, by degrees would take television out of the perceived Stone Age and into the modern world appealed to her. So did the notion that a notoriously conservative network would give her creative freedom. But Moore was unsure and initially unwilling to commit, fearful that any new role might suffer in comparison to her character of Laura in *The Dick Van* Dyke *Show*.

Moore turned to her husband, Grant Tinker, with her concerns and found an experienced hand who seemed to have all the answers. Tinker started out as an ad agency executive back in the late 50's when advertisers created programming specifically to promote their product. He was the ideal choice to bridge the gap between money and creativity, a bottom line, dollars and sense guy with a progressive streak that saw the potential for greatness in giving creative types their head without corporate interference. Those traits served him well when, in 1961, he joined the

NBC network where he was instrumental in creating such endearing shows as *I Spy*, *Dr. Kildare* and *The Man From UNCLE*. He went to New York in 1966 to head up NBC programming but left after a year to return to Los Angeles (and to be with Moore) where he worked developing programming for Universal. If Tinker did not have the answers Moore was looking for then nobody would. As it turned out, Tinker did have the answers.

Tinker suggested that Moore and he should form their own independent production company, called MTM Enterprises, and bring in their own writers and producers to limit the possibility of network interference despite CBS's insisting that the couple had a free hand in all creative decisions. Moore was in agreement and MTM Enterprises was born.

The couple turned to writers Jim Brooks and Allan Burns to get the creative wheels moving. Tinker was familiar with the pair through their award-winning realistic, issues-oriented approach to the series *Room 222*. He liked their modern, progressive approach to a television medium that, admittedly, had grown lethargic. Tinker called up Brooks and Burns and gave them their marching orders. Something bold, something new and something very much in keeping with the times.

The timing for what was shaping up as a radical departure from the staid nature of television could not have been better. Woodstock had brought the notions of social and political upheaval to the fore on a massive commercial and cultural scale, aided and abetted by a thriving second wave of the women's movement in which the pill and the women's independence in a social and sexual way brought the notion of divorce as not only a taboo subject but part and parcel of the options that were opening up for women. In its own way, *The Mary Tyler Moore Show* was suddenly shaping up as a conduit for political and social change on the small screen. And as they began to hash out the outline of *The Mary Tyler Moore Show*, both Brooks and Burns sensed the possibilities and the challenges.

Their first outline would produce the most daring results. Mary Richards would be a 30 year-old divorcé. It was an immediate cause to consider. Outside of feminist and liberal circles, divorce was a philosophical and societal ogre, causing various shades of dread, especially along the television superhighway. Going into 1970, there had never been a female divorcé, or any divorced member of either sex, in a prominent position in a series. Adding to the conundrum was that Moore was so cemented, relationship-wise, in people's minds to *The Dick Van Dyke Show* that there was some legitimate concern, almost immediately discarded, that viewers would truly believe that this new character was actually Laura and that she was now divorced from Rob.

Laughable, but there again this was television. Of seeming minor concern by comparison was that Mary's new job would be an assistant to a newspaper gossip columnist, a job that would most certainly be considered condescending to more liberal minds.

Once they had their pitch in place, the first stop was Moore and Tinker's Hollywood Hills home. They were quite thrilled with the concept they had hatched for the actresses' big television comeback. However,

Brooks and Burns knew the reality of the situation. It was a risky idea, one that many would consider the next big evolutionary step up from *The Dick Van Dyke Show*. Tinker had liked them, and that had gotten the two creators through the door. Now all they had to do was please Moore.

Brooks and Burns immediately got down to business, introducing Mary Richards as a sweet and smart young girl from Minnesota who, on the occasion of turning 30 and being divorced, was on her own in a big city, trying to carve out a personal and professional life. It would be both bold and funny in the way it mirrored real life issues at a time when women were facing these selfsame challenges in the real world.

Moore got it immediately. She knew the realities of being 30 and divorced. She loved that Mary's odyssey would be fresh and the source of endless possibilities. It all seemed very new and exciting. Needless to say, Tinker's enthusiasm was not far behind. "I hired you because you did stuff that seemed to be in the real world," Tinker said in an *Emmy Magazine* article. "And that's what I want this to be."

Having rallied Moore and Tinker to their side, Brooks and Burns knew that their next hurdle on the road to *The Mary Tyler Moore Show* would be their toughest, sitting across from a table full to the brim with old, conservative white men who were the ultimate gatekeepers at CBS, not that CBS was the lone culprit in the networks trying their damnedest to keep the status quo. All the networks, to a large extent, seemed quite content to trot out the same old warhorses—the police, doctor, medical dramas and obvious and slight variations of the classic sitcoms—

seemingly an insulating bubble to what was going on in the real world just outside the television screen.

Consequently, it did not take long for the pitch meeting to transform itself into a surreal indictment of the concept of divorce and CBS, at least at the executive level, to stray far from the clichés that had served them so well in the past. Michael Dann, CBS' program director whose position at the time was shaky, began the inquisition by asking, as chronicled in *Emmy*, "You want to divorce Mary?" To which Brooks and Burns replied, "Yes, we want to divorce Mary."

Objections rained down on the pair from all around the table, citing acting legends Doris Day and Lucille Ball as the way they thought Mary Richards should be. The meeting was rapidly going downhill when a research department man stated, in a quote from *Emmy,* "Our research says American audiences won't tolerate divorce in a lead of a series any more than they will tolerate Jews, people with moustaches and people who live in New York."

Brooks and Burns returned to Los Angeles and a follow-up meeting with CBS vice president Perry Lafferty. Easily as hard a sell on the question of divorce, Lafferty did warm to the idea of a show more daring and, seemingly reluctantly, told Brooks and Burns that they would have to return to New York and convince Dann. The follow-up meeting in New York with Dann was a very ugly version of a Mexican stand-off. The CBS suits were defiant on the subject of divorce. By the time the second meeting had concluded, the unspoken consensus seemed to be that Brooks and Burns were about to be taken off the show. But they had one thing going in their favor.

Tinker liked the two creators and under no circumstances was he interested in firing them. But, perhaps more important than Tinker's opinion, was that he was married to Moore who had loved the original premise. Tinker was willing to reconsider the divorce angle if Brooks and Burns agreed but anything beyond that was out of the question. Brooks and Burns agreed to re- examine the whole issue of divorce and would ultimately brainstorm a new concept in which Mary was now no longer a divorcé but would still be 30 and single after recovering from a break-up. Rather than, somewhat predictably, shuttling her off to a big city like Los Angeles or New York, she would now get a job in a local TV newsroom. Throw in character driven co- workers and an equal set of new friends and the reworked *Mary Tyler Moore Show* suddenly had teeth that even the most prudish CBS executives could not argue with.

And at the end of the day, with Tinker and Moore thoroughly on board with the changes, there was little naysayers could do. In the *Emmy* story, Fred Silverman, who at the time worked with Dann as CBS vice president of development, acknowledged as much when he said, "Moore and Tinker wouldn't back down. They knew exactly what they wanted to do and they were going to do it. After that, the network threw its hands up."

Nineteen seventy would be a landmark year for the women's movement in America. On August 26, The Women's Strike for Equality celebrated the 50th anniversary of women's suffrage in the US with a nationwide strike and series of protests that reached across America. The US Congress enacted Title X of the Public Health Service Act, the only American federal program devoted to family planning services nationwide. The country began 1970 taking up sides on the issue of abortion that would, ultimately be decided early in the decade when the Supreme Court would rule on Roe v. Wade and plans were being made for what would for many become the bible of the women's movement, *Ms. Magazine*. This would also be the year that legendary feminist leader Bella Abzug would be elected to the US Congress while uttering the slogan, "A women's place is in the house."

Lost in the shuffle of history being made in the women's movement, a little-known television series called *The Mary Tyler Moore Show* was taking its first tentative steps. It would be a show that would be for laughs but, on a much more, subtle level, that would define for a television audience what it was to be 30, single and female in the world of 1970 that was suddenly coming of age.

"This is what I wanted to do," Moore recalled in *Emmy*. "I would have loved that this [her character] would have been divorced. But this is great."

Chapter Ten
Mother and Child Disunion

By 1969, Moore was in a seemingly can't win situation. Despite her best efforts, her fledgling movie career was floundering. And when she would retreat into a personal life, she found that the relationship with her son Richie was, likewise, going downhill.

Both Moore and husband Tinker had proven to be very professionally driven and demanding of the actress' son, even more so in the wake of Moore's miscarriage. From the outset, Richie appeared often an after-thought in Moore's life. He was rarely photographed with his mother and sheltered from much of the publicity associated with Moore. When she was on the comeback trail with *Dick Van Dyke and The Other Woman* and the ramping up of *The Mary Tyler Moore Show*, she was spending less and less time at home and, by association, less time interacting with her son. And she would often recall that what interaction she had with her son was less than pleasant.

"I demanded a lot of Richie," she said in her memoir *After All*. "I was responsible for a lot of alienation."

Not that her shortcomings as a mother were a rare

occurrence in the world of celebrity parents. The history of Hollywood families is littered with the consequences of celebrity offspring trying to measure up and compete with ego-driven star parents. And while Moore never shied away from her failures as a mother, they were often couched in a defensive and, yes by degrees, selfish picture.

In an AOL.com interview, Moore laid the blame directly at the feet of her mother who, she claimed, "I emulated my mother's behavior toward me." In *Parade*, she laid much of the blame for her perceived inconsistent parenting style at the feet of her father. "I did bring to my life some of my father who was very controlling and very remote."

But at the end of the day, much of Moore's failure as a parent could only be laid at the feet of Moore, as she confessed in an interview with Barbara Walters. "I think I was as good a mother as I could have been. But I think that I was so wrapped up in myself, as you must be at such a young age. Being 18, 19 is still a very precious growing period and there I was with a baby who was also demanding full attention. I didn't get the enjoyment out of being a mother than I could have."

For Moore, her inattention to her son ultimately boiled down to career vs. motherhood with career usually winning out as she explained in *Parade*. "I still feel as if I weren't a good enough mother. I didn't break any rules. I didn't cause my son any pain. But I was working a lot and I wasn't there a lot."

The result, as it pertained to Richie, was inevitable. By the time *The Mary Tyler Moore Show* was going into production on its first season in 1970,

Richie had become extremely distant around his mother and stepfather and began having trouble in school. By all reports, when Richie spent time with his father who had remarried and continued to lead a traditional, non-Hollywood life, he was a much happier and quite the normal boy. When Richie's father relocated to Fresno, Ca. for a new job, his parents came to the quite amicable conclusion that Richie would be better off living with his father. Richie would move out of his mother's home and in with his father in 1971. Moore knew it was the right thing to do.

"I just didn't invest enough time in Richie," she told Charlie Rose. "I was never at home."

Chapter Eleven
Stealth Feminist

Mary Tyler Moore Show co-creator James L. Brooks concedes that the show would turn out to be an important addition to the political and social discussion of the late 60's and early 70's. But he moved to correct the at-large impression in an *Esquire* interview when he stated, "*The Mary Tyler Moore Show* came along at the beginning of the women's movement. But I don't think the show was seminal. I think its timing was seminal."

Brooks makes a good case that the television industry was, indeed, coming around to a more progressive way of thinking. The notorious Hayes Code, which almost from television's inception had forced television couples to sleep in separate beds when on screen, was abandoned in 1968. And less than four weeks before the official unveiling of Mary Tyler Moore's new show, nationwide protests under the Women's Strike for Equality brought women's rights in countless arenas to the fore.

Dr. Elana Levine, Director of Graduate Studies in journalism, advertising and media studies at the University of Wisconsin/Milwaukee, told Revelist that, "*The Mary Tyler Moore Show* was a perfect convergence of the right people at the right time. The television industry was realizing that American women and the expectations we had of their place in society was changing. *The Mary Tyler Moore Show* was the first sitcom to show a woman making strides in a male dominated world."

And co-creator Brooks, in conversation with *The Hollywood Reporter*, acknowledged that the timing could not have been better. "We've just had the women's march and you can't not think of the qualities that Mary had. The timing was extraordinary because it was just at the point where the women's revolution was starting and some of our stories came from that. But we knew from the beginning that it was important that the show not just become a polemic of the times and that we just do the character of Mary."

There was a definite feeling out process involved in the days leading up to shooting the first episode of *The Mary Tyler Moore Show* between Moore and the show's creators Brooks and Burns would meet regularly and informally. To the casual observer of those meetings it was often considered more social than business but, as Moore explained to *USA Today*, a chemistry that would carry on through the entire run of the show was coming together.

"The writers got to know me and, on that, they went to work," she recalled. "I was probably very close in personality to Mary Richards at that point and we agreed that they would never sacrifice character for the sake of a laugh. A lot of subjects that our writers took on were new. They [the storylines] had not already been seen 105 times. We came in at a very good time." Along those lines, Moore, in an interview with Larry King, acknowledged that, at the end of the day, "The show was written honestly. There were never any manufactured laughs."

But there was inner turmoil on Moore's part. One could not get very far into a description or a press interview without considering that *The Mary Tyler Moore Show* was the next logical step from *The Dick Van Dyke Show*. Moore treasured her days on *The Dick Van Dyke Show* but insisted that *The Mary Tyler Moore Show* was a different animal. And she would do everything in her power to drive that point home.

At Moore's insistence, she wore a brunette wig during the first season of the show to make it clear on a subconscious level that she was not still Laura Petri. She also quashed the idea that it would be an instant ratings attraction to have Dick Van Dyke appear as a guest star in an early season one episode. "In those days, Mary wanted to distance herself from what she had done before," related Herbie J. Pilato, founder of the Classic Television Preservation Society, in a *Fox News* story. "She wanted to leave *The Dick Van Dyke Show* behind her."

As did show creators Brooks and Burns, especially when it came to writers. The late 60's into the early 70's had produced a slow but steady influx of female writers in television and, in their infinite wisdom, Brooks and Burns felt that a sitcom about a 30ish single woman making her way in a professional and largely male-dominated world would make sense having women create her stories with a modern, real world sensibility. They immediately found two writers very much cut from the Mary Richards mold, Treva

Silverman and Susan Silver who had been knocking around the Hollywood screenwriting circuit for a time, had made some notable progress and were looking for their next big break.

The Mary Tyler Moore Show made an immediate, albeit quiet, debut. CBS was still not totally convinced that the show would work and so, despite a cautious commitment for a full slate of first season episodes, the executives mentally filed a 13 episode cut off point should the show fall flat with viewers and in the ratings. And, initially, things were marginal at best. The show was slotted opposite one of the reigning old school comedies, *The Don Knotts Show*, and the early ratings were only passable. And there was some initial blowback, from both men and women at the way Moore's modern woman and her storylines were being portrayed.

But one thing was certain from the opening episode in which Mary arrives just out of a long relationship looking for a new job and a new life in Minneapolis, there was a sense of creative tension and excitement in the air. Silverman proved particularly adept at crafting stories that emphasized her personal life and, from season one, episode two, those would, for many, be the episodes that made Moore a standout. To wit: the episode "Today I Am A Man" in which Mary and Rhoda invite their dates back to Mary's apartment for a get together. There was the hilarious "Divorce Isn't Everything" in which Mary and Rhoda join an organization of divorced people in order to get a travel discount. "Howard's Girl" cast a quasi-slapstick element when Mary's budding romance runs afoul of her boyfriend's parents who insist that she belongs with their other son. Silver also managed to add a different angle to Mary's personal and professional attitudes with the episode "A Friend In Deed" when an old friend of Mary's from their summer camp days turns up as WJM's new receptionist and wants to be Mary's friend again.

With the new show came the expected onslaught of press coverage. This was not particularly new for Moore who had been the subject of some media scrutiny on *The Dick Van Dyke Show*. But for all intents and purposes, Van Dyke was the star and subject of the lion's share of the coverage. *The Mary Tyler Moore Show* was a completely different story. Her name was the title of the show and so the tidal wave of newspaper, magazine and television reporters who descended on the show were all targeting her. Moore did her best to deal with the onslaught of questions but would often acknowledge that it was difficult to be on for the media and still be herself, especially when an interviewer's observations might be striking too close to the bone like the day she read that one interviewer had observed that Moore's face was starting to show some wrinkles.

Critics were quick to descend on *The Mary Tyler Moore Show* with a variety of opinions. Some offered up the notion that it was an important bit of stealth feminism in which heretofore undisclosed social and political declarations of the women's movement were being played out and discoursed in a normal, everyday manner by people so subtle that their simple conversations and exchanges were ultimately as important as protest marches and angry demands. People seemed to be getting the show and, in Mary Richards, they were seeing their own hopes and dreams.

It was not long before Moore was bombarded with the questions of the show's implied feminism and her place in this expanding sitcom universe. It was questions that often left the actress fumbling for an answer. But, when confronted by the *Associated Press*, she seemed to have found it.

"Mary Richards certainly was never a character that I had to develop when we were doing the show. Everything I did was by the seat of the pants. I reacted to every written situation the way I would have in real life."

Midway through season one, the reaction to the show remained mixed with the CBS executives still contemplating a mid-season cancellation notice. But cooler heads prevailed when it was decided to try *The Mary Tyler Moore Show* at a different time slot with another powerhouse, *The Beverly Hillbillies* as a lead in. The switch worked with the show ending the season at a respectable No. 22 in the all-important Nielsen rankings and assuring that the show would be back.

The Mary Tyler Moore Show would hit its creative stride over the course of the next three seasons, showing that it was, indeed, possible to mix real world issues, both personal and professional, and marvelous comedic moments into a successful viewing experience. The ensemble cast was an object lesson in how an entire cast could have its singular and collective moments, all within the central worldview of the star of the show.

The best episodes during that three-season period are impossible to pin down. Everyone had a different opinion and it would be next to impossible to come down on the side of anyone as truly one of the best. But when the dust settled there were some fine examples of *The Mary Tyler Moore Show* world that would be acknowledged as classics by a wide variety of critics.

"Put on a Happy Face" showcased a brilliant comedic turn by Moore when Mary is nominated for a prestigious award and everything seems to go wrong. "The Good Time News" is one of the more message heavy mixtures of funny and feminism as Mary pushes for a raise after she discovers she is being paid less than her male counterparts. "The Dinner Party" is the occasion of formally introducing Sue Ann Nivens as a cast regular. It also signals yet another hilarious chapter in Mary's ongoing and disastrous attempts at throwing a party. "Better Late…That's a Pun…Than Never" is every television journalist's nightmare. Lou suspends Mary after she accidentally reads a joke that she wrote on the air of an obit of a not-yet-dead celebrity.

By the end of season 4, *The Mary Tyler Moore Show* had reached its zenith as the oft cited founding father of real world television comedy. The Emmys had long since sat up and taken notice and the feminist movement remained alternately annoyed and praise worthy as they dissected each line of every script. Amid the scrutiny and the inevitable questions that had surrounded a show that had certainly defied both the odds and the hard and fast rules of traditional television, Moore, in an interview with *Archives of American Television*, was once again asked to make sense of it all.

"It was never a stand on the soapbox and shout kind of show. It pioneered but it pioneered without being self- conscious."

Chapter Twelve
The Movement Looks at Mary

Get Virginia Carter talking about *The Mary Tyler Moore Show* and Moore in particular and, in her own quiet and measured way, she will talk your ear off.

Carter, in her own low-key and subtly humorous way, is the character of Mary Richards before there was a Mary Richards. As a single woman, Carter, much like her television counterpart, has gone out into the world and accomplished a lot. Multi-degreed in the area of math and physics at McGill University and the University of Southern California, Carter became the only physicist at Douglas Aircraft Corporation and would go on to do advanced research for The Aerospace Corporation. By the early 70's, Carter had become an active feminist and would eventually become the head of the Los Angeles Chapter of The National Organization of Women (NOW) where, among other accomplishments, she was an active participant in getting The Equal Rights Amendment passed.

Carter came of age in the women's rights movement right about the time *The Mary Tyler Moore Show* burst onto the pop culture scene both a popular success and the source of much controversy; much of the later issues crossing swords with the likes of NOW and other feminist organizations.

"It was a time when everybody had something to say," Carter told the author in a 2017 interview. "Some of the people were very upset with the show, while some were very confident in what was taking place. But it seemed that they were all taking aim at the same target. Which was Mary Tyler Moore."

Which, reportedly, made Moore the target of being recruited as a spokesperson by feminist luminaries and, in particular, Gloria Steinem. Carter feigned ignorance of that oft told story. "Did Gloria approach Mary? Not to my knowledge. I knew Gloria very well. She had a tremendous capacity for outreach and networking. Frankly, I would be very surprised if she didn't. Her ability to outreach in those days was huge."

Carter saw *The Mary Tyler Moore Show* as promising on a number of issues that were high up on NOW's multi- tiered agenda. "My impression of the show was very positive at that point. Until the show came on, it seemed the main thing that women had problems with in the world was sex. But Mary was addressing that issue, on primetime television, in a fairly upfront way for the time, as well as a whole lot of other issues. The important thing for the time was that Mary Richards had a voice."

Carter continued. "She was an independent woman. She had a position in the workforce. Mary had a male boss but she was independent and confident enough to step up to the boss. And she was confident enough in the world that she spoke up when she felt she was right. It was a new way of being for women in the workforce."

In looking back on the run of *The Mary Tyler Moore Show*, Carter paints a picture of wonderful 'moments' that were reflective of the feminist energy abroad in the emerging sense of real world wants and desires. "The show was being progressive by television standards. Mary became the role model for women who were independent, taking care of their own needs and who did not depend on a husband.

"The idea that a woman would go to her male boss and demand a raise was a critical moment for women. To that point, women in the real world would never think of doing such a thing. When Mary confronted Lou, it was a wonderful moment."

Carter conceded that 'wonderful and important moments' did not necessarily translate into universal applause. "For feminists, it would have been very liberating. For housewives, there was probably a degree of uncertainty. I don't think society was as open as it should have been in those days."

But at the end of the day, Carter would acknowledge, almost as an understatement, that *The Mary Tyler Moore Show* "was quite unique."

"Mary Tyler Moore was on the cutting edge of what was beginning to happen. Whenever you get people talking, no matter their opinion, it helps and The Mary Tyler Moore Show definitely got people talking."

Chapter Thirteen
There's Gonna Be a Showdown

Midway through what would be a seven-year run, *The Mary Tyler Moore Show* had arrived as a bonafide hit for the CBS Network. Although the show would never be No. 1 in the Nielsen ratings, it was always a consistent top 20 or higher performer. By the second season, the show had become a perennial Emmy nominee and award winner, with Moore gathering her own top honors. Which, not surprisingly, put the show, increasingly, in the crosshairs of the women's movement and, particularly, The National Organization of Women whose primary spokesperson and defacto leader, Gloria Steinem, had recently launched *Ms. Magazine*.

While many were grateful for the sentiments *The Mary Tyler Moore Show* were injecting into the television universe, author Armstrong related that the feminist movement at large was not thrilled with the show or Moore.

"At the time, the feminist movement wasn't super enthusiastic about the show," explained Armstrong. "Many feminist leaders criticized the show for not being feminist enough. Mary called her boss 'Mr. Grant' while everybody else called him Lou. To their way of thinking, neither Mary nor the show went far enough in standing up for major feminist issues. The show would become an icon of empowerment over time but, during its run, at the height of the women's movement, it was not necessarily seen that way."

And as many observers hoped it would be, Moore's flowering as a front and center feminist was often sidetracked by Moore herself. Although in private she would often come out, nominally, as favorable to the feminist causes of the day, when it came to public statements on the matter, she would often come across as ambivalent, as witness this quote from the book *Mary and Lou and Rhoda and Ted*.

"I think women are okay. I mean I like women. But I know a lot of people that don't like them. That's partly women's fault. They allow themselves to be put down, put back in the kitchen when the men are talking. In my mind, I can see a lot of the new thinking about the female role but, emotionally, I'm not there. I tend to defer to my husband, to accept his dominant role. And there are certain things I'd rather talk over only with other women. Unisex looks like it's here but I hope we never lose our sexuality. I wouldn't like that at all."

Moore was more upfront and by degrees defiant of Steinem and the more aggressive elements of the feminist movement when she discussed her differences with the NOW leader in an article in *The Federalist*. "Gloria Steinem thought that I was 100 percent on the Betty Freidan train and I really wasn't. I believed that women had a very major role to play as mothers and that it was very necessary for women to be involved with their children. And that's not what Gloria Steinem was saying."

It would turn out that not every feminist had Moore and her character in the crosshairs. No lesser light than women's icon Betty Friedan was highly supportive in a 1978 article as reported by the *Minneapolis Star Tribune*. "This was such a happy, human image of a woman as an independent person that several generations of young and not so young women stopped suffering if they didn't have a date on Saturday night."

Friedan's remarks aside, it would be remarks like Moore's and thinly veiled critical put downs of her character in the show as 'white feminist' that, going into 1975, would put Moore and the show in a can't win situation in the eyes of more liberal/feminist observers.

"Again, we need to distinguish between the character and the person," Armstrong told the author. The character of Mary Richards reflected many of the values of the movement, but Moore herself did not identify as a feminist. I do know that she resisted being a spokesperson for the women's movement. She was not the full-blown enthusiastic spokeswoman that, say, Valerie Harper was.

The feminist movement as a whole was enjoying a breakthrough year in 1975. The United Nations chose that year to announce International Women's Year, which would transform into an annual observance as March 8 was designated as International Women's Day. The US President Gerald Ford would climax this year of recognition by issuing Executive Order 11832, creating a national Commission on the Observance of International Women's Year. Nineteen seventy-five would also be a pivotal moment for both the women's movement and *The Mary Tyler Moore Show*.

The Conference on Women in Public was equal parts political and social call to arms and zealous pep rally. Literally a Woodstock for feminists, the conference highlighted such women's movement all stars as Gloria Steinem and Virginia Carter and no subject in the known universe could get away from deep discussion and animated discourse as it pertained to women's rights.

Carter, the former leader of the Los Angeles chapter of the National Organization of Women, recalled in a conversation with the author that many of the conference attendees were wound pretty tight. "Those in attendance were more not the average housewives. They were already in a frame of mind to want more than *The Mary Tyler Moore Show* was offering at that point. Some of them were downright angry. I remember I was getting angry. But you had to start somewhere and Mary Tyler Moore was on the cutting edge of what was beginning to happen."

Including *The Mary Tyler Moore Show,* in the conference seemed all important .The conference organizers knew representation by somebody connected to the show would be a hot button issue as they searched far and wide to find somebody from the show to the show to attend who would be brave enough to defend the show from the almost certain slings and arrows. Against his better judgment, co-creator Brooks, who readily acknowledged that he is not the most comfortable public speaker, agreed to step into the fire. And the women of NOW seemed poised to light the match.

In introductory remarks, Ambassador Anne Armstrong exhorted the women in the audience and around the world to "go public." Women are now in centerstage. You owe it to the movement not to shun the spotlight." Steinem took to the mic, among other things, highlighting the importance of television in forming and informing public attitudes towards women. Steinem noted that "Mary Tyler Moore agitated for equal pay and got half of what she asked for. It was a very pop cultural compromise." All the while, Brooks was, internally, most likely shaking in his boots.

The co-creator's remarks made a spirited defense of the fact that *The Mary Tyler Moore Show* was very much moving with the times and had been very realistic in depicting the challenges of women in the real world. The question and answer session that followed saw Brooks defending and responding to particulars of the show as they related to the women's movement. The question of what to call her boss, Mr. Grant or Lou, was of particular interest to the audience as to how Mary Richards had evolved into a feminist heroine were discussed and debated, in a spirited and occasionally antagonistic back and forth. Brooks ultimately gave as good as he got in the best possible way and, given the tenor of the evening, came away with a few supporters. Among them, Virginia Carter.

In a conversation with this author, Carter recalled that night when she said, "I remember Brooks being very forbearing. That night was a tough situation for anyone to be in. I felt a certain degree of admiration for the way he held it together and did not come apart at the seams. In hindsight, I don't know if I would have been able to."

Chapter Fourteen
This is the End

By 1975, television networks were starting to get it. And no one would be a bigger recipient of the rise in realism and thought provoking content brought about by *The Mary Tyler Moore Show* than producer Norman Lear. Lear was well aware that television comedy with a real world edge was not going to go away and, over the life of *The Mary Tyler Moore Show*, created *All in the Family*, *Sanford & Son*, *Maude*, *The Jeffersons*, *What's Happening* and *Mary Hartman, Mary Hartman*, all far from the formula created by Brooks and Burns, yet all taking bits and pieces of the show's vibe and daring and taking it to the next level.

Going into what would be the final seasons of the series, *The Mary Tyler Moore Show* had seemingly arrived in a state of grace when it came to the feminist movement. And nobody could argue that the series had, through a quite organic process, become just about everything on the women's movement's wish list. Behind the scenes, *The Mary Tyler Moore Show* had become a groundbreaking, equal opportunity employer with a total of 25 women writers working regularly on the show and, in many cases, advancing to producer and other writing credits.

What had only been hinted at, at the time was that, with the show's consistent emphasis on Mary's career arc, Moore's character had finally arrived as a full-blown role model for countless women growing up in a world outside of the fantasy of television. *The Mary Tyler Moore Show* had hit on all the touchstones, women choosing career over marriage, that having casual sex was okay and that making one's way through day to day life did not always result in a fairy tale ending.

After the political and social challenges propagated by the show in its first five seasons, the final seasons of the series, by comparison, appeared to fall into an overriding pattern of failed and confusing relationship storylines and the craziness that evolved around inter-office politics and more of an emphasis on gags and shtick. Not that the show had seemingly lost its mojo but, rather, it had transformed into a different creative state in which seemingly small moments had taken center stage over message stories and daring bits. But that did result in some classic Mary Tyler Moore Show moments.

"Chuckles Bites The Dust," which in the minds of many observers, was the best episode of the series, gave Moore some of her finest comedic moments as she loses it during the funeral for the show's clown. "Look At Us, We're Walking" would be the Mary asks for a raise episode that struck at women's rights in a solid bit of message and comedy. Much was made of the potential inter-office romance with episodes "Mary Richards Falls in Love" and "Lou Dates Mary."

But it would remain for both the comedy and the poignancy of "The Last Show" to put the capper on the series.

Behind the scenes, Moore had grown into a comfortable place when it came to the show and her character. She had grown to, instinctively, know what was right and wrong for Mary as she related to her television audience. An example of this being the episode in which Mary has her tonsils out. As originally conceived by Brooks and Burns, Mary was, in fact, getting a tattoo removed but Moore put a gentle end to that storyline when she said that a good Catholic girl would not have a tattoo.

Not surprisingly, over the run of *The Mary Tyler Moore Show*, Moore had come to acknowledge that the character of Mary Richards was very much a part of who she is, acknowledging in several interviews including a report in *The New York Daily News* that she was "Seventy-five to 80 percent like Mary Richards." To the point that, when it was announced that *The Mary Tyler Moore Show* was going off the air at the conclusion of season seven, Moore, as reported in *The New York Daily News*, announced "that it was her idea [to end the show] and that it was time for them to move on."

For Moore, it was a convenient excuse, her character falling on the metaphorical sword and being stoic in the name of it all as she hinted at in a conversation with *People*. "The producers and the writers wanted to go on to other things and, at the time, it was incumbent on me to express absolute belief that this was the smart thing to do, to go off while we were ahead and on top."

But Moore had not told the truth. For Moore it was all charade and the truth hurt her on an even more painful level.

"But it wasn't my idea at all," she said. "It was producer Allan Burns' and James Brooks' and it [their decision to end the show] scared the hell out of me. I was crumbling inside. I didn't want it to end. So I said it was my idea… and then I'd go back to my dressing room and just sob my eyes out."

Chapter Fifteen
From Minneapolis with Love

Roseburg, Minnesota. A small, conservative town well off the beaten track. In fact, Roseburg is so far out of sight that it only exists in the imagination of the most diligent imaginations. Roseburg is where Mary Richards came from.

And according to *The Mary Tyler Moore Show* co-producer Brooks opined in a *Time Magazine* interview, where Mary ultimately arrived at all boiled down to football. "We chose Minnesota [ultimately Minneapolis] when one of the writers began talking about the strengths and weaknesses of the Minnesota Vikings."

Ultimately Minneapolis would be chosen for Mary's final landing and, logistically, it seemed to make sense. Los Angeles and New York had pretty much been played out as far as television series locations were concerned. Then there was that Midwest weather. More often than not, it was cold and bordering on inhospitable. But for the types of storylines and visuals the show had in mind, it was perfect.

Except for some trips to Minneapolis to shoot B roll establishing shots and what would become the famous shots of Mary walking local streets and joyously throwing her hat in the air, *The Mary Tyler Moore Show* would be shot entirely on Hollywood soundstages. But once word began to leak out, nobody could doubt that *The Mary Tyler Moore Show* was middle America through and through.

On the surface, Minneapolis seemed the ideal setting for a situation comedy with progressive undertones. Long an easy mixture of conservative and liberal attitudes, the residents were most likely thrilled at the notion of a network television series being filmed against the backdrop of their town. As it would turn out, The Mary Tyler Moore production crew would ascend on Minneapolis several times to shoot stock footage of the city and would find much that was in keeping with the vibe of the show.

The house where Mary lived. In the script it was 119 North Weatherly Avenue, Apt. D. In real life, the address was 2014 Keenwood Ave. The owner of the home would quickly grow tired of the tourists and the traffic that was a by-product of the show's popularity and would try to get the series to move Mary into another dwelling. But the production company would not budge and, by 1973, the owner would take matters into his own hands by putting up Impeach Nixon signs all over the front of his house. By 1975, there would be a story change in which Mary would move into a new apartment, which would be the then recently constructed Riverside Towers.

For the theme and credit sequences in which Mary is seen strolling along the lake, the production company found the perfect section of the city's' Lake of the Isles, while a sequence of Mary shopping was conceived on Nicolet Ave. next to the IDS Crystal

Court, a food/mall complex. During the show's opening montage, Mary is seen having lunch with an old friend. Stepping in as the old friend was Moore's husband Grant Tinker. Nobody seemed to recall the name of the restaurant at the time but, currently, the eatery goes by the name of Basil's. When the show cut to an exterior shot of the WJM newsroom, the shot would often include a tall building. In the show, it had been dubbed The Snyder Building. In reality, it was the Midwest Federal Savings & Loan.

Part of the sequence in which Mary is shopping at a grocery store was filmed in another Minneapolis landmark, Kowalski's Market on Hennepin Ave. The first season sequence, which shows Mary driving toward Minneapolis for the first time, took in segments of Interstate 494 and the Highway 65 spur as well as momentary glimpses of the Minneapolis skyline and such recognizable landmarks as the Doubletree Hotel in nearby Bloomington and the Basilica of St. Mary.

Easily the most memorable bit of footage shot was the moment that Mary, standing in the middle of a busy intersection, joyously tossed her beret into the air. As chronicled in interviews with Moore in both *National Public Radio* and the *Archive of American Television*, Moore recalled the day that legendary bit of B roll was shot.

"We didn't know what we were doing. We were just there to grab a lot of footage. It was really a spur of the moment idea. We were out there [next to the Nicollet Mall], in the middle of February, freezing. They just wanted shots of me in action. It was in front of a department store and they said, 'Oh look here! Run out into the intersection and take your hat,' which

I held in my hand, 'and throw it in the air as if this is the happiest moment of your life.' And I did and that was it."

The Mary Tyler Moore Show would return to Minneapolis in 1973, primarily for the purpose of reshooting the show's opening montage. Among those residents who happened upon the filming was Minneapolis resident Randall Munson who, at the time, was working in Dayton's department store, on the very corner where the original Mary throwing her hat in the air sequence was filmed. Munson recalled that day and other memories of the shoot in a 2017 conversation with the author.

Munson related that by the time The Mary Tyler Moore Show returned to Minneapolis, Moore and the show had essentially become the town's favorite daughter. "When they came in 1973, it was a big buzz, everyone was excited. There was local pride and a heightened interest in the show."

Munson let on that, with the town, by this time, very familiar with The Mary Tyler Moore Show's progressive storylines and attitudes but that there had been nary a hint of an uproar. "I didn't sense any reaction like that [to the show's storylines]. To the people in town, the show was funny and interesting and it did catch on for the local scene. But I didn't sense that there was any concern or uproar because of the social implications of the show."

Munson recalled that he had joined the crowd of locals watching the filming and he laughed as he remembered the moment that fate stepped in and made him a local celebrity.

"Word got out that the film crew was outside so I

went across the street to the IDS Tower. I joined the crowd of spectators as they shot Mary Tyler Moore coming out of an elevator. Some people volunteered to be extras who walked through the scene. Then the director said they needed another businessman in the shot. He walked over to me and asked 'would you be willing to help us out?' After thinking it over for a half of a nanosecond, I agreed and was positioned next to Mary Tyler Moore in the elevator."

Munson remembered that he had been positioned directly in front of Moore in the elevator. After a couple of rehearsals, the cameras rolled on a simple shot that would, nonetheless result in numerous takes and the opportunity to make small talk with the actress.

Munson and Moore literally rubbed shoulders for more than a dozen takes of the elevator door opening and its occupants, including Moore and Munson, walking out in different directions. Given the time between takes, Munson made small talk with Moore. "She was nice and smiley and chatty," he recalled. "I was directly in front of Mary. It was cool to be right next to her and to have a chance to talk to her. She was focused on getting the shot right but she was not chatting away. She would answer my questions about how things were shot. She was very pleasant."

Munson related that the film crew was shooting in different locations for several days and he was able to observe much of what was going on. One scene, in particular, offered up a hint of Moore as still, even at this stage of her life and career, was still very much an innocent. It was an outdoor scene and Mary with in a Minnesota Vikings football jersey and she was being asked to wash a car. She suddenly got a funny look on her face and said, 'How do you wash a car?' Such a normal thing as to how to wash a car was completely unknown to her. The director finally came over and said put this [wash rag] in the bucket and slosh it over the car."

Munson proved a quick study of Moore while observing the filming and having a brief conversation with the actress. "She had the same smile, the same pleasantness, whether she was in front of the camera or just talking between takes. She did not show any aloofness or impatience. Looking back on all the things that had gone on in her personal life, I kind of felt sorry for her. Being a superstar, I'm sure she was not able to get out of the bubble and be what most people would consider a normal person, living a normal life."

There had been some concern that The Mary Tyler Moore's liberal leaning storylines might not set too well with the local residents. But, to the contrary, the individuality of Moore's character met with almost universal praise for Mary's individuality and every woman stance. Upon further investigation, it should have come as no surprise.

Minnesota had a long history of actively supporting and pursuing women's rights on a number of fronts and, coinciding with the run of *The Mary Tyler Moore Show*, had been particularly active. In 1977, numerous solidarity activities resulted in Rosalie Wahl being named the first woman to the Minnesota Supreme Court. That same year, various women's groups quite literally took to the street in a successful attempt to draw attention to an adult theater district that had sprung up on the south side of one Minnesota district that ultimately shut it down. In 1970, a group called Women Against Male Supremacy picketed a Minneapolis fashion show on a number of charges including newspaper advertising segregation.

Following his stint as an extra, Munson was very much on pins and needles waiting for the new season of The Mary Tyler Moore Show and, for what he hoped would be his brief chance at celebrity as an extra standing next to Moore. He was savvy enough about how the film industry worked to have prepared himself for all his scenes ending up on the cutting room floor. The new season opened and as he turned on his television, he hoped for the best.

The scene with Munson flickered on the screen. Munson was overjoyed. There he was with Mary Tyler Moore in an elevator…

Sharing a moment.

Chapter Sixteen
Peaks and Valleys

Moore seemed quite content going into 1976. *The Mary Tyler Moore Show* was chugging along like the proverbial well-oiled machine. The ratings remained quite good and the accolades were continuing to come thick and fast. But Moore was beginning to get a bit restless. She was quite content playing Mary Richards. But she sensed that the show was nearing its final season and the thought of suddenly being left without work played on her insecurities. She knew that there were choices to be made.

Moore wanted to remain in television. It had become her comfort zone, as Moore explained to entertainment columnist Marilyn Beck. "As a performer, I can go to my grave happy now. I've done everything I've wanted to do." But no small amount of ego and the suddenly renewed spirit of adventure would finally steer her slowly but surely into new and exciting opportunities.

Consequently, Moore continued to jump at every opportunity. While finishing out the string on *The Mary Tyler Moore Show*, she willingly stepped before the camera to help CBS and her production company spin off supporting characters Rhoda and Phyllis into their own individual series. Between 1974 and 77, Moore, as Mary Richards, would make six guest appearances on Rhoda and two guest shots on Phyllis. In 1974, Moore also worked behind the camera of the CBS mini-series *The American Parade* which was created to celebrate the United States Bicentennial. The actress gave a spirited narration to the episode entitled "We The Women."

Moore continued to be a cautious feminist in her personnel and professional life, moving into what many would consider a stage of quiet liberalism. But she would put her cards, literally, on the table when she agreed to star as NBC News correspondent Betty Rollin in the 1978 movie for television, *First You Cry*, the true life story of Rollin's emotional battles with breast cancer. For Moore, the film would be a breakthrough, allowing the actress long known for her comedy to shine in a fully drawn, dramatic tour de force. *First You Cry*, which would go on to win several Emmy awards, was not only a professional breakthrough but also an insight into her emotions as a woman.

"I cared a lot about that project," she told *Interview* magazine. "I felt from having read the book it was based on that if it [breast cancer] were to happen to me or somebody close to me that I would handle it much better. I wanted the film to reach many more people which I felt could only be done through television."

Moore began to mentally cast around for a new direction. Landing another series, based loosely on her Mary Richards' character seemed a fairly safe option that some network would, most certainly, jump at. But for Moore, it seemed like too much of the same. In her more thoughtful moments, the idea of an old-fashioned singing/dancing variety show, a concept that many felt had begun to grow stale by the mid 70's, might be the way to go.

Moore began letting it be known around town that she was interested in a variety show concept and was soon approached by writer-creator Jack Good who had become the hot new kid in Hollywood based on a successful special he had created for the television rock band The Monkees.

Moore related to *United Press International* that "When Good came to me with this idea, I told him he had carte blanche, without any structure or guidelines from me. His idea was a unique, no holds barred musical happening…

It was called *Mary's Incredible Dream*.

Picture if you will a surreal take on a stock variety show format in which Moore drifts in and out of dreams in multiple characters as she contemplates and interprets the creation of man through the singing of pop, rock and classical standards. Adding yet other levels of incredulity are the moments when Moore, who drifts in and out of a dream-like state to dance in odd costumes with Ben Vereen. Looking for a capper to what was ultimately an indescribable acid trip? How about the group The Manhattan Transfer doing a cover of The Rolling Stones' song "Sympathy For The Devil?"

And perhaps the most condemning aspect of *Mary's Incredible Dream* landed directly in Moore's lap. Long lauded for her dancing and singing ability, the *Incredible Dream* highlighted Moore's suddenly diminished and mediocre skills at both. By the time, *Mary's Incredible Dream* landed at CBS's pretesting stage, the consensus was that, as a straight variety show, it was an unmitigated disaster. The network called for some last minute reshoots that would make it clear that this was only a dream and, thus, soften the critical blows that were sure to come.

Yes, it was that kind of show. It aired on television only once in January 1976. And as Moore would recall in her memoir *After All*, "As it was presented, it [*Mary's Incredible Dream*] met with hostile response from both critics and audiences. We were tarred and feathered. I find bits of fluff in the odd shoe or coat pocket to this day."

But Moore would be resilient in the face of this failure on a large scale not long after *The Mary Tyler Moore Show* came to an end when she decided to give the musical comedy yet another go round with the one hour special *How to Survive the 70's and Maybe Even Bump into Happiness*. The storyline, in which Moore, in a light-hearted examination of herself and her Mary Richards character within the context of the ramifications of surviving the title decade, was modest in its concept and execution and, with the disaster that was *Mary's Incredible Dream* still fresh in her memory, it seemed, to observers, the ideal transition to easier footing. Which was made much less stressful by the addition of some name performers in support mode, Dick Van Dyke, Harvey Korman and John Ritter among others, all made appearances in a series of skits and song and dance numbers. The show promised to be a relevant and biting look at the times but, while it came up a little soft on both counts, *How to Survive the 70's and Maybe Bump into Happiness* was decently received and reviewed and, emotionally, seemed to put Moore on track for the next step in her post-*Mary Tyler Moore Show* odyssey.

Despite dire industry predictions of a dying industry warhorse, the hour-long musical variety show, Moore was convinced otherwise and had already convinced CBS that a weekly variety hour entitled *Mary* would work. The result was that *Mary*, which featured the earliest efforts of such future stars as David Letterman, Michael Keaton, Swoozie Kurtz and veteran Dick Shawn, debuted on September 24, 1978 to a resounding thud.

Mary, while a spirited attempt at being a much tamer version of *Saturday Night Live* and the old-style variety hours of better days, failed, often embarrassingly, to capture the spirit and spontaneity of either. There would be occasional glimmers of hope in the scattershot nature of the comedy sketches, musical guests and dance numbers but ultimately, *Mary* fell immediate victim of bad ratings and even worse reviews and the plug was, mercifully, pulled after the third episode.

Things were most likely tense between Moore, and by association Tinker, and the CBS executive suite at that point. CBS knew that not being able to get Moore her post *Mary Tyler Moore Show* hit was weighing on everybody and their respective egos. Needless to say, the press was quick to point out that the failure of everything Moore had attempted was doomed to failure because the audience was not willing to let her portrayal of Mary Richards go and was reluctant to see her as anybody else.

Author Armstrong insisted that Moore had already come to terms with her place in television history and was, most likely, comfortable moving on and attempting other things. "I have found that many actors are pretty well adjusted about it. They understand that they are lucky to have had a huge hit and to be well known for something. She seemed happy to revisit *The Mary Tyler Moore Show* in TV appearances. Her public appearances did not indicate that she resented the show's success or her connection to it."

But with everybody inclined to give it one more shot, a radically retooled version of *Mary*, entitled *The Mary Tyler Moore Hour*, was unveiled early in 1979. The show, essentially a hybrid part sitcom/part variety show, in which Moore plays a television star and the inherent trials and tribulations of putting on a weekly variety show. The premise was simple, perhaps too simple, which was why the production coppered their bets by introducing the angle of a name guest star whose appearance is an important part to that week's storyline. Among the stellar stars of the day to make an appearance were Lucille Ball, Ken Howard, Gene Kelly, Johnny Mathis and Dick Van Dyke.

By television standards of the 70's, *The Mary Tyler Moore Hour* was competently put together, the storylines were not complicated or cluttered and the star of the week notion worked for the most part. But the bottom line is that Moore's star power still did not stretch much beyond Mary Richards. Consequently, the show struggled to attract viewers for 11 weeks before CBS called it a day.

If Moore was disappointed at this latest cancellation, she did not show it. In fact, shortly after the cancellation of *The Mary Tyler Moore Hour*, she announced that plans were already in place for a new sitcom for the upcoming 1980 television season.

Chapter Seventeen
Once Upon a Time in 1973

The feminist movement was going full bore in 1973. In January, The Supreme Court case Roe v Wade hearings struck down most state restrictions on abortion. An equally important but less publicized Supreme Court decision, Frontiero v Richardson ruled, later in 1973, that denying military benefits to male spouses was illegal sex discrimination.

And although it would not take a Supreme Court decision to make it so, 1973 was also the year that *The Mary Tyler Moore Show* scored a major victory against the Hollywood establishment when it was proudly announced that a third of the 75 writers regularly employed on the show were women.

Entering its third season, *The Mary Tyler Moore Show* had reached an unbreachable level of acceptance. While never hitting No. 1 on the television ratings, the numbers overall could not lie. The show was now a perennial winner as both an entertainment and progressive-thinking show that had been accepted by the masses. Professionally, Moore was on top of the world.

Personally, her life was in shambles.

By 1971, Richie had left the chaotic life surrounding the celebrity of his mother and had moved to Fresno, Ca. where his father and his new wife had relocated for his father's business. Richie thrived in his sudden introduction to middle class normalcy. He was more social, his grades improved and, by his senior year in high school, was already considering going to college.

But when his father was unexpectedly transferred out of town because of business, Richie and his father had a very serious sit down conversation. Richie wanted to stay in Fresno and finish his senior year. His father, recognizing his son's personal growth and maturity, agreed that it was best that his son was ready to be on his own and so Richie was left alone in Fresno for his final year of high school. For a time, it seemed that leaving Richie on his own was a good idea. But then he fell in with the wrong crowd and, in February 1973, Moore found out firsthand how far her son had fallen.

"It wasn't until a frantic, sobbing Richie called home, begging for help in dealing with a cocaine dealer who had threatened to kill him over some unpaid debts that I realized the extent of tangles that were now my son's life," she painfully recalled in her memoir *After All*.

For Moore, that phone call would, for yet one more time, force her to deal with the guilt of being an inattentive mother and she was suddenly frantic in trying to make amends. With Tinker's help, she found a doctor who specialized in treating young people with drug problems which, by the 70's was a growing concern in young Hollywood. Moore struck a deal with her son. She would get him help if he came back to Los Angeles and lived with her. It was a fragile, emotionally scattered and quite frail looking Richie who reentered his mother's life. Moore took one look at her son and prayed that she had gotten to him in time.

Richie was returning to a home life that was far from perfect, thanks in large part to Moore's already full-blown alcoholism that, she now readily admitted, had its roots in her days on *The Dick Van Dyke Show*. But she would admit years later that she was able to hide her excessive drinking from most of her friends and co-workers, often by calculating how much the people she was with were drinking and matching them.

In her memoir *After All*, Moore reflected on the fact that "My alcoholism started building when I was in my late teens and it became my strength during the years I was on *The Dick Van Dyke Show*. For me, alcoholism tended to bring to the fore hostilities and resentment."

Moore reflected on her alcoholism in her early days in a conversation with Larry King. "With alcoholism I tended to drink because I was angry or I drank because I was sad or because I was just so happy I wanted to celebrate."

And she was quick to point out in *After All,* that her drinking would often cause difficulties in her marriage to Tinker. "We would have these inane arguments over dinner about things I couldn't even remember about, things I could not remember the next day."

But Moore's drinking was not the only problem in what, after a decade of marriage, had turned into a relationship that seemed all business and no love and that was rapidly disintegrating. Moore painfully recalled in her autobiography *After All* the night it all came to a head.

"One night in 1973, after dinner and an argument, he [Tinker] said that he thought we should separate and that we had poisoned the marriage and that, perhaps, 11 and a half years was all we had in us."

Moore's reaction was the equivalent of a shot between the eyes. "My face flushed and my mouth went dry," she recalled in *After All*. "I headed to the bathroom, dropped to my knees and began crying and screaming 'no!' over and over. It was the tantrum I was never allowed as a child."

Moore came out of the bathroom and, having regained her composure, told Tinker that she wanted him to have his things out of the house in two days. Tinker went to their bedroom, followed shortly by Moore who climbed into bed with him. "I asked him if he would put his arms around me for a while. He did."

The separation lasted six weeks. For Moore, it was agony. She was missing Tinker terribly. Which was why when Tinker offered a truce, Moore moved back in with him. On the surface, things appeared back to normal. And in the worst possible way they were…

…Because the silence continued, as did the drinking.

Chapter Eighteen
The Great Silence

In hindsight, moving back in with his mother and Tinker did not appear to be the ideal prescription for Richie as he attempted to get off drugs and get a new lease on life. And it was not Richie's fault. Because what he was witnessing was a lot of unhappiness.

Despite the reconciliation, things quickly returned to the unhappiness that had initially driven them apart. Moore and Tinker had soon returned to drinking which, in turn, led to loud and often angry arguments. When business matters literally forced them to speak to each other, they would manage but, otherwise, the silence in the house remained deafening. But through it all, Richie managed to get his life back together and return to his senior year of high school.

Moore would acknowledge her son's turnaround in her book *After All*. "Richie got himself straight and finished high school. I wasn't able to attend his graduation that was such a triumph for him because I was busy taping my show."

Moore's guilt continued when it came to her inability to fully connect and be there for her son. She would often exclaim to her trusted circle that her son was "rudderless" but she could have just as easily been describing herself and her seemingly impossible task of keeping her rapidly deteriorating marriage together. In all fairness, Moore and Tinker would often make an effort to make things better. Often during a break from the never-ending arguments and drinking, there would be moments of clear headedness in which they would sit with each other and try to figure out what to do.

They tried counseling on several occasions but neither seemed to have the patience to see the process through to any sort of conclusion. As always, any setback in their relationship would, inevitably lead to more drinking and more uncontrollable lashing out. The actress, during those dark periods, allegedly contemplated suicide.

Moore, during one of her more candid moments in *After All*, described how, when drinking, she would often indulge in making her alleged death wish a reality in a bit of Car Russian Roulette in which Moore, while often intoxicated, would get into her car and drive up and down the streets of her neighborhood, barreling through stop signs and into the path of oncoming traffic.

"In case there's any doubt about my acute state of alcoholism and the insanity it produced, I can recall with sickening clarity than on more than one occasion, I played Russian Roulette with my car without any concern for my own safety and the safety of others."

Moore seemingly saw the high drama in this incident, perhaps preferring to couch certain moments in her life as part of a less painful theatrical production then, what to her, was a much more hurtful reality. A case in point being the aforementioned car incidents in which Moore seemed the mental director of what was going on at the moment, which she offered up in an excerpt from her memoir.

"Upon hitting the wall with Grant, I'd vent my furious frustration by storming into my car, slamming it into reverse and out into the street. I'd hit the accelerator and run each stop sign in Brentwood until I reached Santa Monica Blvd. It was the certainty of a collision at that juncture that would finally bring me to a halt and the tears would reduce the force of my anger."

While Moore and Tinker played out what seemed the inevitable disillusion of their relationship, much of Moore's family life seemed poised to strike at her already fragile psyche. Especially when it came to the presence of her much younger sister, Elizabeth Ann Moore.

Much of the relationship between the two Moore sisters was predicated on the anomaly of Elizabeth not only being a late in life child, born 19 years after her older sister but, by virtue of being born on March 20, 1956, she was born the same year Moore's son Richie was born and was actually three months older than Richie. By the time Elizabeth was only a few years old, Moore was already hard at work on *The Dick Van Dyke Show* and, not surprisingly, the relationship between the two siblings was less of sisters and more like an older aunt and a younger niece. In any case, the relationship was fragmentary at best, largely due to Elizabeth's relationship with their father, which was quite loving compared to what passed for the relationship between Moore and her father. It was a situation in which Moore, over the years, harbored some resentment, often citing that Elizabeth's relationship with their father was quite different than that of Moore and her father.

With Moore's busy schedule, the two sisters rarely got together and Moore would end up getting information about Elizabeth from a distance. What little is known is that Elizabeth, by that time she turned 21, was in a steady, live-in relationship and doing reasonably well. But that would change in 1978 when, according to Jason Bonderoff's book *Mary Tyler Moore*, Elizabeth reportedly broke up with her boyfriend. The report continued that, Elizabeth, emotionally distraught at the break-up, went to her parent's house where she found her mother drunk. Elizabeth went to her Aunt Bertie's house. What happened once she entered the house that night was never quite clear but, when her aunt awoke the next morning, she found Elizabeth dead in a bed. The coroner's initial result was that Elizabeth had died of an overdose of alcohol and painkillers. Elizabeth's death was ruled a suicide. A distraught Moore reportedly insisted that it could not have been a suicide.

The death of Moore's sister added more pain to an already tattered existence. Her drinking continued and the emotional distance between Tinker and herself seemed more pronounced. There seemed no reason for the couple to stay together but, surprisingly, they persisted, hoping against hope that there still might be a chance for them.

While Moore balanced professional highs and personal lows throughout much of the 70's, the women's movement appeared to be on a definite upswing in the social and political consciousness of the country.

In 1975, a precedent was set for rape victim's rights of self-defense in sexual assault cases when Joanne Little was acquitted of the murder of Clarence

Alligood after Alligood had assaulted Little. In 1978, over 100,000 people marched on Washington D.C.to force politicians to extend the time limit to ratify the Equal Rights Amendment. And by 1979, the National Organization of Women was increasing its presence and influence, drawing both radicals and middle class housewives to the cause to the tune of more than 100,000 registered members.

Moore would soon be challenged in the deepest, most personal way when Robert Redford picked her to star in the film *Ordinary People*. The role Redford offered Mary was light years away from anything she had done to that point. It was a taut, dark and painful drama in which Moore plays the mother of a well-to-do family whose oldest, and favorite son, died in a boating accident, who is attempting to deal with the trauma of his death while attempting to deal with a second son who had just been released from a psychiatric institute following a suicide attempt and a husband from which she has drawn distant. Moore was excited that Redford would consider her for the part. But she was also frightened.

The role would force Moore to explore a dark side that, in her private moments, she felt she harbored but was not certain if and when she would ever bring it out. Her feelings about the role quickly found the actress drawing a comparison to her long-suffering and dysfunctional relationship with her parents, especially her mother.

It was at this moment, with Moore at her most personally and professionally vulnerable, that she would have an affair.

Now on set romances are nothing new. The

history of film is rife with them. But what made this dalliance all the more enticing was that she would later admit that her fling went directly against a conservative, stringent and religious upbringing that had guided her through the first 40 years of her life. And as she explained in *After All*, she was willingly giving up that ghost.

"The Catholic in me was convinced that I was committing a mortal sin. On the other side of the ledger was the undeniable affirmation was that I was an appealing woman that I had forgotten."

Moore refused to name the other half of this on-set romance to the end. She would concede in a moment of candor that the mystery man was only the third man she had ever had sex with. And she would acknowledge in *After All* what an eye opening experience it turned out to be. "I met him on the set of *Ordinary People* after the shooting had begun. When he touched me for the first time with such intense passion and curiosity, I thought I'd die from pleasure. In our lucid moments, we reminded ourselves that this was a heartfelt, yet temporary phenomenon of location shooting. He had a long-time commitment and wasn't interested in changing that life."

The affair ended with the conclusion of filming on *Ordinary People*. Moore returned to Los Angeles where she would soon discover that Tinker, likewise, had been having an affair, literally behind her back, allegedly with his 22 year-old secretary. The couple's dual infidelities would be the last straw in their already deteriorating relationship as they lived out the last few months of 1980 in silence.

Moore would soon be the recipient of this

feminist march in an unexpected personal and professional way. *Whose Life is it Anyway?* Was a daring acting challenge for any actor. The idea of a sculptor who is paralyzed from the neck down following an accident whose often stark and humorous asides to wanting to die collide while doctors debate whether to keep the patient alive or shut down life support had the makings of a career making role.

Actor Tom Conti portrayed the bed-ridden character when the play opened in London. The early reviews were only passable and so, when the play relocated to Broadway, the company, admittedly an aside to the growing feminist movement, decided that the role would be turned on its head and an actress would play the lead role.

Moore was drawn to the notion of tackling easily the most difficult role of her career. Could she keep an audience interested and enthralled while laying on a bed for two hours, being allowed very little mobility and essentially acting from the neck up? Could she deal with the rigors of an eight performance a week schedule? There were easier ways for an actress to go in 1979 but easy was not what Moore wanted.

Whose Life is it Anyway?, with Moore in the lead, would run a total of 96 performances between February and May 1980. The play became an immediate cause celeb among critics and became an issue performance of some stature. Moore's performance was deemed powerful, honest and forthright and instantly gave her the breakthrough role that went a long way toward shaking her from *The Mary Tyler Moore Show* comparison. Because, quite simply, there was none.

And in the process, Moore, had, whether she agreed with the notion or not, suddenly became a flag waver for the feminist movement amid glowing stories in the likes of *Ms*. and *McCall's* that pointed to Moore's performance in *Whose Life is it Anyway?* as an overall breakthrough for women. Moore would be awarded a special award at that year's Tony Awards.

And that success would signal the start of a new chapter in Moore's life. With Moore's professional life now on an upswing, the actress and Tinker, in typical Hollywood style public fashion, divorced in late 1980.

Shortly after the Tony Awards, and now newly single at the age of 42, Moore decided to relocate to New York. And to live alone.

Chapter Nineteen
Alone Again

Moore was awakened from a sound sleep on October 15, 1980. The phone was buzzing. Moore had long ago speculated that late at night or early morning telephone calls never meant good news. As she would recall some years later in her autobiography *After All*, this day would be no exception.

"The phone rang," she recalled. "It was Grant. He said 'If you're standing, you should sit down.' I told him 'I am sitting.' He said 'It's Richie. He's dead.' All I could think of to say was 'What do you mean?'"

Tinker would later painfully acknowledge that moment when he told a *UPI* reporter "Calling Mary was the most difficult thing I ever had to do."

Moore's heartache would be preceded by a gratifying series of highlights. Her well-received, nuanced performance in *Ordinary People* had resulted in nominations and wins in such prestigious awards organizations as the Academy Awards and The Golden Globes. Moore was particularly heartened that the more laudatory reviews indicated that her role in *Ordinary People* had been a legitimate career breakthrough in which the actress had finally been allowed to breathe outside the bubble of her landmark television portrayals. And one that would allow her decision to relocate to New York all the more promising.

Moore would often acknowledge that being 43, suddenly single and about to embark on a great adventure in New York was an exciting and enticing prospect. "I had never experienced any of the situations around which *The Mary Tyler Moore Show* had been based," she related in her memoir *After All.* "She was an independent woman, carving out a career, finding her way in a strange city, making new friends and doing exactly what she wanted. And now I was that woman, doing what I wanted. Alone!"

Moore's transition to New York life was a methodical exercise. Her first step was to rent a house on East 64th Street in Manhattan. It was one of those comfortable places that was close enough to everything, yet ideal to the prospect of her suddenly being on her own. The next step, and one borne of pure vanity was that Moore, in an attempt to shave some years off her appearance, had some 'work' done on her face.

Moore eased into the single life. She had friends and was regularly spotted at New York social gatherings. And, to her surprise, she was finding being single in the big city only an occasional shock to her system. Moore was determined not to rush into any kind of new, serious relationship and to what degree she was dating during those early days in New York was open to conjecture. But she would admit on occasion that she would sometimes wish she had a man on her arm and was in some kind of committed relationship.

Moore's new life in New York could not keep her away from a very old demon. Her drinking had long since evolved into a full-blown case of alcoholism and, in the classic sense, Moore found herself often drinking alone. A typical scenario would play out often in those early months. After a day of being out and about, she would typically return to her house and, promptly at 5:30 p.m. she would begin playing with her new toy, a margarita maker. She would then spend the next few hours drinking, watching television and skimming through magazines. It was a way to salve the fear, insecurities and the aloneness of the next chapter in her life.

Richie's life had been on a definite upswing since getting into rehab and getting off drugs. He had finished high school and was doing well in college. He was in a committed relationship, living, platonically, with two female roommates and working at the *CBS Network* as a messenger and had even managed to get a few small acting roles.

And then there were the guns.

Richie was an avid gun collector, hunter and target shooter. But when it came to guns, he was nothing if not responsible and careful. Which was why his two roommates and his girlfriend never gave it a second thought that there were guns around the house. Which was why on the night of October 14, family and friends were shocked to discover that, shortly after hanging up the phone after a long conversation with his girlfriend, Richie was reportedly cleaning a shotgun when it went off, hitting him in the face with what would be a fatal blast.

"It came out of nowhere," Moore related of the

incident years later in her book *Growing Up Again: Life, Love and, Oh Yeah, Diabetes*. "He was doing so well."

Typical of the Hollywood press at the time, early reports of Richie's death wildly speculated that the young man's death had been a suicide, yet another sad ending to the child of a famous celebrity. But evidence almost immediately emerged, coupled with the insistence of Moore and those who knew Richie, pointing toward a tragic accident.

Moore was in a state of shock, inundated with reporters bombarding her with personal and prying questions, wanting details about easily the saddest day of her life. Moore would retreat into autopilot when circumstances forced her to deal with the incident in the media. Some phrases would tumble out in emotionless monotone with surprising regularity.

"It came from out of nowhere," she recalled of Richie's death in an interview with *The National Ledger*. "Unfortunately, there were terrible rumors that Richie had killed himself, but it was an accident. He was a gun collector. He was cleaning one of his guns and it went off and shot him in the head."

Wracked by sadness, Moore was, nevertheless, focused on the task at hand, which was to prepare for her son's funeral. It would be a private ceremony, with a small gathering of family and friends. The last thing Moore wanted was the press descending on the somber proceedings and turning her private time into a three-ring circus. Moore would painfully remember the moment when she cast her son's cremated remains into the Owens River.

"The water was clear and high as I knelt over it,"

she recalled in her book *After All*. "I opened the container and emptied it [his ashes] into the running water. What was meant to be a prayer became an outraged demand. 'You take care of him,' I screamed at the sky."

The consensus among those closest to Moore was cautious optimism in the wake of her son's death. Not surprisingly, she was somber, sad and prone to sudden outbursts of tears. Among those expressing hopeful sentiments were her soon-to-be ex Tinker who acknowledged in a *UPI* interview that, "Mary is holding up pretty well. She has moments of terrible sadness. But she's strong. She will be fine. But it's going to take time."

With her divorce from Tinker looming along with the emotional impact of Richie's death, Moore quite literally shut down and went into total seclusion. She would see or talk to few in her inner circle and would rarely leave her home. Moore would enter therapy and that would prove helpful in helping her to deal with the death of Richie as well as her guilt over her perceived failings as a mother.

News of Richie's death immediately went around the world and would touch the hearts of Moore's fans. to the extent that the actress eventually received more than 6000 letters of condolence. Moore was touched by this outpouring of sympathy and took it upon herself to sit down and write out a personal response to every one of the letters.

It was a cruel twist of fate that, after rave notices in *Ordinary People*, Moore was not emotionally ready to work again in the face of the offers that were most certainly coming her way. No one is certain what roles

Moore may have turned down in the two years following Richie's death and her divorce. But by 1982, Moore was psychologically ready to deal with reality and the fact that an actress had to work.

She accepted a co-starring role opposite Dudley Moore in a tear jerker romantic comedy entitled *Six Weeks*. By studio standards this tale of a mother whose daughter has leukemia and only six weeks to live, was a bit shop-worn by studio standards. Audrey Hepburn, Faye Dunaway and Jacqueline Bisset had all passed on the role of the mother that Moore would finally accept.

The film was fairly pat and predictable but Moore was more than capable of pushing the appropriate emotional buttons and *Six Weeks* would go on to do okay box office. Moore would continue to test the waters in a cautious manner over the next two years, returning to her love affair with television with a pair of decent, well-acted and totally underappreciated movies for television, *Heartsounds* (1984) opposite James Garner, and *Finnegan Begin Again* (1985) with Robert Preston. In the former, Moore played the wife of a doctor whose own malady puts him in direct conflict with the very institution he has always championed. In the latter, she is one half of a later in life relationship between two mismatched people who are, alternately, dealing with issues of their own.

What few people would realize was that Moore, who shot the two films literally back to back on tight, demanding schedules, was physically breaking down. Those in the know assumed that it was the continued effects of her Diabetes that were making her ill. Others, in more hushed tones, speculated that Moore was continuing to drink to access and that was beginning to haunt her physically. But the reality was that she was just feeling lousy and that nobody knew for sure what was the cause.

For those who have seen them, *Heartsounds* and *Finnegan Begin Again* showcased Moore as continuing the solid dramatic chops she had exhibited in *Ordinary People*. Although she would rarely admit as much, Moore seemed determined to at least temporarily lay aside the notion that all she could do was variations on Mary Richards. But truth be known, these small professional steps were minor in Moore's universe at that point. Because by 1985, she was already on to more important things…

Chapter Twenty
Love and Rehab

The women's movement had made great strides in the years after *The Mary Tyler Moore Show* had gone off the air. By the early 80's, women's rights had become a legitimate and, in many corners, respectable aspect of society and culture. There would be the occasional in fighting on certain aspects of the women's movement, spats between organizations and ideologies were common, but the conceit as women as an organized, powerful and influential force to be reckoned with, had emerged as a very real aspect of society and one that would continue to resonate with the emerging hopes and aspirations of upcoming generations of women.

And no less important to the rise of women as a powerful force was the impact that *The Mary Tyler Moore Show*, less than a decade removed from its seven-year run, had proved a driving force in the worlds of many who had spent their Saturday nights alone watching the show and, most importantly, taking from it the things that would drive them into highly respected and rewarding careers and lives of their own.

Actress/comedian Tina Fey echoed the at-large

influence of *The Mary Tyler Moore Show* in conversation with *The Sunday Times* when she stated "Mary Tyler Moore was a working woman whose storylines were not always about dating and men. They were about friendships and relationships which is what I feel my adult life has always been about." During a 1997 interview with Moore, Oprah Winfrey could barely contain herself when she gushed, "You have no idea what you've meant to me. You were one of those women who was a light." Veteran news reporter Andrea Mitchell was succinct when she acknowledged in a tweet that "Mary Tyler Moore influenced my career more than any other TV role model."

During the early 80's, Moore would rarely acknowledge the accolades or, for that matter, be very public. Emotionally, it appeared she had pulled into a shell. By her own account, she remained a "functioning alcoholic." Whether by choice or design, Moore refrained from doing any other work after the two movies for television. If there was a bright spot in these seemingly difficult times, it would appear that she had made peace with her parents after years of emotional distance and would now visit frequently and be attentive to their needs.

Which were significant. Moore's mother had recently suffered a stroke and her father had an abdominal aneurism. In an attempt to boost their spirits, Moore told them that she would send them on an all-expenses paid trip to Europe if they both recovered. They did and, reportedly, the trip went a long way toward cementing their relationship.

Unfortunately, upon their return, Moore's mother suddenly fell ill with a severe case of bronchitis. When a frantic Moore, called her mother's regular doctor and found that he was unavailable, she was referred to another doctor who was on call that day.

Dr. Robert S. Levine saw Moore's mother and would, some days later, see her in a second treatment session. All of which gave Moore ample time to be around the 29 year-old cardiologist. Moore could sense that he was serious, intelligent and very cute. It may not have been love at first sight, but there was some feelings in the air. Levine, in an interview with *People*, would recall that the feelings were reciprocal.

"After I had seen her mom a second time, I said to Mary, 'If there's an emergency just get in touch with me.' And she said, 'does loneliness count?' and I said 'yes'."

Moore and Levine went out on a dinner date a few days later. Shortly after that they officially came out as a couple in a very public way. The news brought more than its share of naysayers. The fact that Moore was 15 years older than Levine brought out some snide remarks about Moore's 'boy toy' and that there would be nothing serious or long lasting about the relationship. But, as the couple continued together, even the cynics had to admit that Moore and Levine were starting to look like the real thing.

Many in Moore's inner circle saw the difference. The smile on her face was real. She appeared more relaxed. It was a sure bet that Moore had fallen quickly and genuinely in love with this truly kind and caring man.

Emanuel Azenberg, who produced *Whose Life is it Anyway?* assessed the relationship this way as quoted in *People*. "There's no question they are in love. They both have too much integrity to stay with the relationship if they weren't."

Longtime friend, actress Valerie Harper, echoed those sentiments in the *People* article. "Moore is filled with joy because she and Robert are friends as well as loving each other. He makes her feel cherished."

Moore and Levine were married on Thanksgiving Eve in 1983.

From the outset, Moore's third marriage appeared ideal. They were together constantly in what had quickly evolved into a fairly quiet, loving existence, comfortable in each other's worlds and social circles and determined to put their spouses' needs and desires above any outside influences. When Moore was working, as was the case with the movies *Heartsounds* and *Finnegan Begins Again*, Levine always cleared his busy work schedule so that he could travel and be with Moore on the weekends. As it would turn out, having a cardiologist for a husband would ultimately provide some added perks.

Levine would later acknowledge that there were signs during the making of those two movies that Moore was in some distress. She was having some moments of weakness, blurred vision and slurred speech. To his practiced eye, these were often symptoms of low blood sugar associated with Moore's diabetes.

But Levine sensed that there might be something else going on. Moore had always been diligent about treating her diabetes symptoms, giving herself three or four insulin injections a day and sticking to a rigid dietary and exercise program. But shortly after Moore had completed the back to back films, Levine began to explore the theory that her latest symptoms might be the result of her chemical imbalance being thrown out of balance by her alcohol consumption, which Levine would often acknowledge as a level of social drinking rather than the raging alcoholism that the scandal sheets had often speculated.

"She was not what you would call an alcoholic," emphasized Levine in a *People* story. "But it was my feeling, shared by Mary's doctors, that drinking was dangerous to her."

To prove his point, Levine began a series of in home tests, beginning with a two week study in which he collected blood specimens from Moore throughout the day and night. He also suggested that Moore cut out all forms of alcohol consumption during the trial period. The results of the tests were that Moore's blood count steadied. Based on the results of the tests, Levine came to the conclusion that alcohol was affecting Moore's body chemistry.

After a consultation of his findings with Moore's other doctors, Levine concluded that it was in his wife's best interest to enter a program that would help her to learn to live without alcohol. Moore readily agreed and would choose the well -known and highly regarded Betty Ford Center.

Moore would often admit that her stint at the Betty Ford Center did the trick but not immediately. Like countless others who have had success with curing their addictions, Moore would admit to a certain amount of backsliding post rehab. But that ultimately her stint at Betty Ford worked.

"Some part of my brain functioned well enough to get me to the Betty Ford Center," she recalled in her book *Growing Up Again: Life, Loves and Oh Yeah, Diabetes*. "My experience at the clinic was a struggle. I somehow knew that it would be. But over a period of five weeks, I grew up some."

Chapter Twenty-One
The Politics of Moore

Mary Tyler Moore's politics and social values were never as cut and dried as the media would often portray them. Point of fact: By the time she turned 18, she was being influenced more by her surroundings and new life experiences than her conservative, Catholic upbringing, in subtle ways that would finally mold her political and societal attitudes as an adult.

Born of a Catholic father and Protestant mother, Moore received a steady diet of religious conservatism that had her speaking a traditional party line when it came to political and social issues, particularly as it pertained to women's rights. But by the time she entered the working world as an actress, she was rounding into shape as a centrist of sorts, willing to go along with the industry's norms right up to the point where she disagreed. And that's when the budding liberal in her would take over.

Her transformation was timely in the sense that, even as far back as *The Dick Van Dyke Show* and the groundbreaking Capri pants incident, she had the support of creative producers who were willing to give leeway in her opinions. However, it would be *The*

Mary Tyler Moore Show that would open Moore's eyes and senses to different opinions and progressive attitudes on a near daily basis. And while Moore was far from the looming march of women's rights, her attitudes in those days were slowly but surely coming around to a more progressive way of thinking. Moore was, by this time, more inclined to listen to both sides of an issue before casting her own opinion.

By the time *The Mary Tyler Moore Show* ended its run, Moore easily qualified, in political circles, as a liberal centrist. But no matter how much she denied it, Moore, politically and socially, was now stuck with the dreaded phrase 'standard bearer.' Author and pop culture expert Jennifer Keeshin Armstrong summed it up succinctly when she offered to Yahoo Celebrity.com that "She [Moore] went in there and made feminism okay."

For her part, Moore after the conclusion of *The Mary Tyler Moore Show*, seemed wrung out with not only her character but also the political baggage it had engendered as she offered in *The Washington Post* and *The New York Times*. "After *The Mary Tyler Moore Show*, I decided I was not going to play any more characters with whom I was totally familiar. "She further insisted that "I can't live with that stuff [he women's rights tag]. I can't carry it around anymore."

That pronouncement may have been a bit premature. Because by 1980, she would be very much in an activist state of mind. President Jimmy Carter had taken time out from a busy re-election campaign to call the actress and express his condolences on the death of her son. The call was quick and to the point. But Moore was touched by Carter's kindness which, in turn, led to her reading up on him and discovering that his platform was very much pro women's rights and that he was a vocal supporter of the Equal Rights Amendment.

It was at that moment that Moore did the unexpected. She came out publically in favor of the liberal Democrat and gave credence to the long held notion that she was actually a moderate liberal. Moore was not into the Carter campaign in half steps. She immediately jumped into the fray by appearing in a commercial in support of Carter's reelection bid. Moore was straightforward, forthright and serious in the commercial. To wit: "Nearly half of this country's women now work outside the home as I do. President Carter wants our women to cut through the years of disdain and dismay to get the guarantees in the home and in the world that they need."

Moore's steps into activist politics did not stop there. After years of dodging feminist overtures, Moore took the big step of joining up with feminist icons Gloria Steinem and Bella Abzug in going to Washington in 1981 to personally advocate for women's rights.

It would be an eye opening moment for Moore. Meeting and working alongside two of the icons of the women's movement opened her eyes to the importance of a movement that she generally agreed with but that had refused to fall into lockstep with. What time the trio spent together during that Washington visit would go a long way toward bringing Moore's concept of the potential and power of women into sharp focus.

Moore would take a major step forward in her personal activism when she decided to be front and center with her diabetes in 1984. This was not the first time Moore had considered taking such a public step. Almost from the moment she had been diagnosed with Type 1 Diabetes during the heyday of *The Mary Tyler Moore Show*, she had contemplated going public with her malady. But she pulled back, fearing the adverse effect letting the world know about her illness would negatively impact the perception of the audience for her show. But in 1984, with a string of personal challenges and breakthroughs buoying her spirits, she, instinctively, felt that now was the time.

Moore began what would ultimately be a 30-plus year crusade to enlighten and encourage those with the disease when she became an advocate and spokesperson for the Juvenile Diabetes Research Foundation, which, in turn, would lead her to the position of International Chairwoman of the organization. In this capacity, Moore would be a regular in the halls of Washington D.C., lobbying Senate and House representatives for funds for diabetes research, testifying in the halls of Congress on the reality of diabetes and the importance of finding a cure, and making regular appearances in public service campaigns. Moore's celebrity status proved a strong adjunct of getting the word out on diabetes, as was her own forthright stories of her own experiences living with the disease.

Moore would take her social activism into other areas. A lifelong animal lover, Moore made herself available to organizations such as PETA and other regional and national humane treatment of animals' organizations.

Nearing the end of the 80's, Moore was now

perceived as a 'born again' Democrat by many political observers. But much of her political and social activism would continue to be of a stealth nature. She would, unbeknownst to many, contribute to left leaning/progressive causes. Evidence being unearthed in PopDig.com which indicated in 1988 Moore had contributed more than $10,000 to various Democratic candidates and causes.

As it would turn out, Moore's politics were like Mercury and would regularly turn on a dime. Well into the 90's and beyond, there would be a political and social shift in Moore's thinking. She had become very conservative or, as she was often want to say, a "liberal centrist.' Moore acknowledged in a *Parade Magazine* interview that she was "finding very few television shows of interest. I watch a lot of Fox News. I like Charles Krauthammer and Bill O'Reilly." She also acknowledged that if John McCain [the senator who was running for President in 2008] "had asked me to campaign for him, I would have."

Moore's slide in and out of politics would ultimately prove a secondary adjunct to a very simple edict the actress had cultivated over the years, as offered in a YahooCelebrity.com piece. "I wanted to be remembered as somebody who always looked for the truth, even if it wasn't funny."

Chapter Twenty-Two
Uptown, Downtown

It had been six years since Moore had worked in television. It had been 1977 and the last episode of *The Mary Tyler Moore Show* since she had last worked in a full-blown, fully scripted situation comedy. Going into 1985, Moore felt it was time to return to that world. In a show called *Mary.*

In this series, Moore played a divorced columnist working on a second rate Chicago tabloid called *The Eagle*. There were the usual set of co-workers and friends and storylines that, upon closer inspection, seemed awfully familiar. It did not take a deep thinker to realize that *Mary* was a not too well disguised clone of *The Mary Tyler Moore Show*.

Mary was almost immediately in a ratings death spiral. The ratings were bad. The scripts were obvious. *Mary* was put on hiatus after the tenth episode for a time slot change and a bit of retooling of the basic concept. But when the 'retooling' was to write two of the characters out of the show and to downplay Moore's character's personal life in favor of more business oriented storylines, the actress, who was seemingly constantly at odds with the producers during the entire run of the show, put her foot down and demanded that the network pull the plug on the show. Shortly after *Mary's* 13th episode, Moore got her wish and the show was cancelled.

But while Moore was disappointed, she was not detoured and immediately cast about for something else. She offered up the need to work in conversation with *The New York Times*. "I've come to a point in my life where I don't have to work. But I work because I enjoy it. I've got to keep the actress in me happy."

Moore would take a fairly unexpected turn between 1985 and 87 when, under the auspices of her MTM production company, she turned to theater production with a largely successful run of original and revival productions that included *Noises Off*, *The Octette Bridge Club*, *Joe Egg*, *Benefactors*, *Sweet Sue* and *Safe Sex*. Moore would prove adept at the day-to-day running of theater productions. But she could not resist the chance to get back in front of a live audience when she took the lead in *Sweet Sue* opposite Lynn Redgrave. The play was particularly challenging in that Moore and Redgrave played two sides of the same character and Moore was encouraged by the very good reviews she received during the 164 performances of the play.

Encouraged to the point that, by 1987, Moore was once again feeling the itch to get back into the television series game. But it would have to be on her terms. The long and the short of it was that her next television attempt could not be another *Mary*, he memory of which still burned uncomfortably bright. In a *New York Times* conversation, Moore winced as she described *Mary* as a shot for shot, plot for plot clone of

The Mary Tyler Moore Show. And she was quick to point out that she was at least partly to blame.

"I'd always been so lucky with my work, surrounded by strength and stability. I never occurred to me to second guess the people I worked with."

Moore was, in her most pessimistic moments, convinced that another television failure might well drive her from working in television forever. At that point *Annie McGuire* entered her life.

Annie McGuire seemed to be taking *The Mary Tyler Moore Show* concept and put it some years into the future. The basic conceit was that Moore's character was on her second marriage, as was her husband. Both had fairly older children from their previous marriages and would mix their day-to-day lives with both comic and serious issues involving their lives together and the interaction with their children and their jobs. Moore liked the idea and was quick to wade in with her own demands. It could not copy the personality or habits of any of her previous characters and no larger than life behavior. In other words, as she explained in a *New York Times* feature, the show had to be real.

"*Annie McGuire* is the first character I've played who is, occasionally, going to have some stains on her clothes. She will take a nap every now and again, screw something up in the house, make a really bad decision with her child and has a sexual vitality that needs to be paid attention to."

Throw in the atypical sitcom filming approach of one camera and the daring of no laugh track and it appeared that, on the surface, *Annie McGuire* might just turn into that long-lost follow-up success Moore was looking for. She was defiant and confident about the fate of this latest attempt with the *New York Times*. "I want to go down knowing I said what I wanted to say and not what somebody else wanted. Through the last TV experience, I came to realize I had to protect myself. Work is my sanctuary, the place I can hide. That's why I'm much more involved in this show."

But despite Moore's mental and emotional sweat equity, *Annie McGuire* seemed doomed from the first episode. The reality was that the show, on any number of fronts, was an immediate critical favorite with Moore's turns as the title character the subject of particular praise. The problem was that CBS, in their infinite wisdom choose to slot *Annie McGuire* at, what many considered, a much earlier and inappropriate time slot for the show. Another issue was that Moore's show had a particularly weak new shot as a lead in. Consequently, not a whole lot of people were watching which translated into *Annie McGuire* being on the bubble of cancellation within the first three episodes. CBS would ultimately keep viewers in suspense, putting the show on temporary hiatus before cancelling it after 11 episodes (three of which were never aired).

In the aftermath of yet another television failure, Moore vowed to those in her circle that she would never return to television again. But shortly after the cancellation of *Annie McGuire*, the opportunity to play Mary Todd Lincoln in the television mini-series *Lincoln* (the television version of Gore Vidal's book) proved too much of a temptation. Moore read everything she could get her hands on regarding Lincoln's wife. Her fascination with the admittedly flawed historical figure proved fascinating to the actress who would translate that fascination into a full-bodied emotional portrayal that, to many reviewers, was the highlight of the mini-series and would result in Moore winning an Emmy for Outstanding Lead Actress in a Mini Series.

That same year, Moore made an appearance in the children's instructional series *Shalom Sesame* which was an anglicized version of an Israeli version of *Sesame Street* called *Rechov Sum Sum* that featured human guest stars and puppet characters from both versions of the show.

When it came to winning awards, Moore, despite her best efforts to expand upon old glories, was never far from honors for her greatest hits, *The Dick Van Dyke Show* and *The Mary Tyler Moore Show*. In 1986, Moore was inducted into The Television Hall of Fame and, in 1988, she received a Lifetime Achievement Award for Comedy from The American Comedy Awards.

While grateful, deep down inside Moore was determined to break new ground.

Chapter Twenty-Three
The Watershed Years

If you blinked during the 1990's, the chances are good that you missed Moore in quite a few things.

The actress was out there and doing, by and large, very good work. But for whatever reason, the big movie roles and all the prospects she had engendered from her work in *Ordinary People* and the very good notices from her theater work were not translating into substantial roles in big budget and well publicized work. Consequently, Moore's desire to keep working was keeping her well below the radar with movies for television, low level theatrical films and a handful of series guest shots.

Moore showed her diversity in 1990, playing against comedic type in a pair of television movies, *The Last Best Year* and *Thanksgiving Day*. In the former, a small dramatic outing, Moore plays a therapist who is reluctant to step in and counsel a young woman who has fallen critically ill. Moore proved quite adept at pathos and inward looking emotions, playing some legitimately taut scenes with co-star Bernadette Peters and playing quite effectively with the admittedly tear jerker aspects of the film. On the other hand, *Thanksgiving Day*, an admitted holiday trifle about a family that comes together at the titular holiday to combat dysfunction and family and business problems in a light-hearted and somewhat predictable outing. Recommended for Moore's comedic outrage and her continued ability to wring good-natured laughs out of a seemingly dire situation.

Anyone who believed that Moore was incapable of doing anything purely evil has not seen a 1993 potboiler for television with the lurid title *Stolen Babies*. Reportedly based on a true story, Moore plays an adoption agency head who is secretly running a black market baby selling scam. Moore lays on the cold, calculating and smoldering evil in a way that will give followers of Moore's trademark light, comedic characters bad dreams.

There would be little for Moore on screen through 1994 except for a guest shot on the television series *Frasier*. But that did not mean that the actress was idle. In fact, Moore, had quickly given up her vow to never do series television again and was, behind the scenes actively prepping for yet another attempt at small screen success.

New York News was shaping up as yet another variation on the whole Mary Tyler Moore motif with some interesting twists and turns. Moore would assay the role of Louise 'The Dragon' Felcott, the hard-bitten, no punches pulled slave driver of an editor-in-chief of a struggling New York City tabloid newspaper called *The New York Reporter*. Moore, essentially a female Lou Grant, seemed rife with possibilities. Moore offered on *The Charlie Rose Show* that she loved playing against type and that she was cautiously optimistic about what she hoped would be a fully developed character.

"Women like that are not necessarily ruthless. They're just so dedicated to the thing they work for, their life's breath, that everything else just falls by the wayside."

Moore hoped for the best. But it was not long before she was getting the worst possible news. CBS, who had a reputation for taking slotting of a new show as an afterthought, had scheduled *New York News* opposite *Seinfeld*, which almost assured that Moore's show was going to get clobbered in the ratings. The actress openly hoped that the network would see enough in the show to give it a fighting chance. But from the first episode forward, Moore would be disappointed. The producers and writers had decided to forgo any deep character elements to Moore's character in favor of a flat, by-the-numbers portrayal. The actress, in those early episodes, seemed to be struggling to get emotion and depth of a character that had not been written that way. Moore was particularly unhappy about her character being written as a tough, unsympathetic and unglamorous woman.

She confessed her disappointment on *The Charlie Rose Show* when she groused, "I didn't feel that my character was being written as fully as she should have been. Not that I wanted more time on the air. But I wanted to understand a little bit about what an editor-in-chief did when she was running a newspaper and there just never seemed to be the time for the writers to address that."

Moore rarely got as upset as she did with the unraveling of *New York News*. The show was typically finishing third or lower in the weekly Nielsen ratings and the producers and writers of the show were seemingly turning a deaf ear to Moore's pleadings for more substance to her character. Finally, she could stand it no more and she went to the network and the producers and demanded that she bet let out of the contract she had with *New York News*. The back and forth negotiations between Moore and the network turned ugly. Moore insisted that creative integrity was the sole reason for her wanting to walk away from the show. The network eventually took the expedient way out and cancelled *New York News* after eight episodes aired (and an additional five went unaired).

Moore was depressed in the wake of the cancellation and once again vowed to never do another television series again. It was a promise that she kept. But in the process, Moore had discovered a sudden urge to explore her dark side and would spend much of 1996 exploring less positive characters in little known or remembered films. Among them was Moore's deep south trashy mother in *Keys to Tulsa*, a neurotic adoptive mother in *Flirting with Disaster*, and a mentally challenged older woman with some deep, dark secrets in *Stolen Memories: Secrets from The Rose Garden*.

It would be an ironic twist on Moore's attempt to shake her Mary Richards image that she would do a voice over in an extremely G rated animated feature *How The Toys Saved Christmas*.

"At that early stage of my life, I was perfectly happy playing myself," Moore reflected in *Entertainment Weekly* on her character experimentation. "But now I think that I've changed so much."

Moore was on a personal and professional journey of discovery as she entered the year 2000 and nobody had a clue as to how things would turn out. Not even her.

Chapter Twenty-Four
Suicide Solution

The assisted suicide/right to die movement continued to gain momentum and prominence in mainstream America in the early 1990's, with many landmark decisions and important moments dotting a landscape that had people on both sides of the controversial issue battling it out in the court of public opinion.

During this period, the American Medical Association would adopt the first formal position that stated, with informal consent, a person could withdraw or withhold treatment for a patient who is close to death. Dr. Jack Kevorkian, who had emerged as a controversial proponent of assisted suicide, assisted in the death of a middle-aged Alzheimer's patient named Janet Adkins. Congress would also take a significant step forward in the assisted suicide movement when they passed the Self Determination Act which required hospitals that received federal funds to tell patients that they have the right to demand or refuse treatment. The right to die movement would enter the commercial publishing arena in 1991 when author Derek Humphry published *Final Exit*, essentially a step-by-step, how-to book on the procedure for ending one's life. The book was an unexpected hit, selling more than 540,000 copies in 18 months and topping several national and international bestseller lists.

It was about the time that *Final Exit* exceeded 100,000 copies sold that Mary Tyler Moore's brother, John Moore, attempted to take his own life.

John had been in the painful throes of kidney cancer for some time and had finally decided that it was time to end his suffering. Secretly, John had been stashing hundreds of painkillers over a period of weeks and, during one of his regular visits to the hospital, had decided that he was ready to go on to the next life. John, according to a detailed account in Moore's autobiography *After All*, had consumed a massive amount of the painkillers when he finally passed out, not in death but, as it turned out, in sleep.

"He had tried the first time and had fallen asleep before he could ingest enough of the pills to end his pain," she sadly recalled, "and they [the hospital staff] had revived him."

Shortly after the failed attempt, John was released from the hospital. His first call was to his sister. His first words to Moore were that he was going to try again. "He felt he could do it again, only this time with improvements. I couldn't argue with him. I just said, 'Please wait for me. I want to be with you.' "

Moore hung up the phone and turned to her husband. They weighed the decisions they would have to make as they contemplated what would be an overnight flight from New York to California to be with John in his final moments. Moore's religious as well as philosophical attitudes and upbringing had always put her feelings about the concept of suicide in a tenuous place. But, with her brother's suffering in the balance, she did not think twice about agreeing to be with him.

Levine readily agreed to be with Moore at her brother's bedside. From an ethical point of view, being a licensed physician and doing what he would be called to do in John's final moments, was difficult. As Moore related in her book "It was difficult from an ethical point of view but he knew he would never be directly involved [in her brother's death.]."

Upon arrival at John's bedside, Moore and Levine, methodically, set about helping John to die. Levine requested that John give him all the pills he had collected for his second attempt at ending his life. As Levine observed, and that was chronicled in Moore's book, the Dialuded, Vzlium, Percocet, Halcion and the ever present morphine that was dripping from overhead into his body, seemed more than enough to kill him. Moore took the pills and ground them into a bowl of ice cream. Levine assured that this time would be successful when he called the drug company and asked for the code that controlled the morphine pump. John's pain was palpable and the couple were doing everything they could to make sure John's suffering was about to come to an end.

The next five hours would be a roller coaster ride into hell. John said an emotional goodbye to his sister and her husband that often had the couple in tears. Levine, at regular intervals, would increase the level of morphine pumping into his body. After a time, the combination of drugs seemed to be working as John, slowly but steadily, slipped into unconsciousness. Some hours later, as Moore and Levine, waited for the signs that John was truly at peace, John suddenly began to cry out in agony. Moore could do nothing as she watched his continued torture play out.

"He was still alive and still in pain," she recalled. "I could not believe he was still living through it."

Moore was living the agony of her brother vicariously, not knowing what to do next. In a state of panic, Moore called her brother's doctor and, literally, begged for help. She was encouraged when the doctor told her that she had exhibited a lot of courage in this situation and that she had not done anything wrong. He would also reaffirm that it was not surprising that John had made another suicide attempt and, like the previous one, it too had failed.

Moore's life for the next three months was put on hold as she watched, often from a distance, as her brother's condition continued to worsen. Doctors could do little to ease John's pain and had eventually resorted to severing the nerves in his arm and a portion of his spinal column. Finally, in December of 1992, John's condition had worsened and Moore and Levine were summoned to his bedside. Moore would remember those final hours in her book *After All*.

"As Robert and I sat holding John's hand, at one point, he told us he had seen God that morning, that he appeared before him and said, 'John, you're going to a place where you'll feel normal.' He was so happy that there was a place called home. Later that night, after a long silence, with just Robert and me in the room, John said, out of nowhere…

…"Mary, let me go."

Chapter Twenty-Five

Bits and Pieces

Moore ended the decade of the 90's on a fairly quiet career note, doing voice over work on an episode of the animated television series *King of the Hill*. Reading between the lines, that choice was an indication that Moore was not on any serious career path. And who could really blame her.

The slow but sure ravages of diabetes were seemingly limiting her from any strenuous filming schedule or career choices. And her physical limitations were also compromised by the fact that Moore, at this point, was, so many years after the fact, still totally typecast as Mary Richards despite some noteworthy and award winning performances that indicated there was a lot more she could do.

If she wanted to. And if the two-hour movie for television *Mary and Rhoda* (2000) was any indication, she was more inclined to return to her seemingly safe and comfortable past rather than stretch for a possible future.

Mary and Rhoda had its roots in a 1997 announcement that Moore and Harper had signed with ABC to reprise their *Mary Tyler Moore Show* roles in a new sitcom for 1998. It was a daring move on Moore's part. Having sold her share of the MTM production company some time ago, Moore was making her maiden television voyage with another network. That *Mary and Rhoda* would turn out to be directly lifted from *The Mary Tyler Moore Show* universe immediately gave rise to the fact that Moore, and by association Harper, were returning to the moment when they were their most popular and successful.

Naysayers and cynics would look upon the choice as a cash grab, pure and simple, that would feed off an audience starved for nostalgia. Others were quick to defend Moore and, by association, Harper who, they insisted, were looking for the best job available and had found it.

The premise of the two-hour pilot was predictable. Mary and Rhoda meet up in New York City after years of estrangement. Mary is now a widow and Rhoda is recently divorced. Both have 20-something daughters who are attempting to find themselves. Long story short, Mary and Rhoda reconcile their differences and Mary invites Rhoda to move into her apartment with her as they attempt to navigate the minefield of jobs, daughters and personal and professional relationships as they close in on the big 60.

The atmosphere on the set of the pilot, shot late in 1999, was nostalgic and relaxed. Although Moore and Harper had stayed in touch, there was still much to reminisce about which made the inevitable compressed TV schedule a lot easier to get through. But below the perceived good times, there was the pressure.

While nobody would readily admit it, Moore, who had nothing to prove at that point in her life and career, did have a string of noticeable television series flops in her closet, another failure could easily tarnish her achievements. But if there was any concern on the actress' part, she was handling it well. She was confident during the shoot, able to slip easily between comedy and lightweight drama and pathos with relative ease.

However, Moore's enthusiasm for the pilot would temporarily override her good sense. In a scene in which Mary is shown running to catch a dog, Moore insisted that she was more than capable of doing the sequence herself rather than using a stuntwoman. The director, well aware that Moore's diabetes and suspect health had reached the point where she could be shaky when it came to physical activity, and was not sure that even doing a fairly simple stunt was a good idea.

But Moore insisted. Reluctantly the director shortly called 'action' on the scene which called for Moore to leap over a barrier while in pursuit of the dog. To the horror of the cast and crew, Moore missed the jump, fell hard and broke her wrist. Ever the trooper, Moore insisted that she be fitted with a removeable cast which she would wear during the remainder of the shoot.

In advance of its airing, the completed pilot was shown to select studio and media types. The response was not good. *Mary and Rhoda* was alternately considered, bland, boring, predictable and forced. Discouraged by the feedback, ABC floated the notion that the show was being retooled and that the network was looking for better scripts. The reality was that by the end of 1999, *Mary and Rhoda* was effectively dead as a series.

But the network was intent on getting some mileage out of the completed pilot and so, in February 2000, *Mary and Rhoda* was aired as a two-hour movie for television. The irony would be that, warts and all, *Mary and Rhoda* drew 17.5 million viewers and while the viewing audience echoed some of the initial complaints, the overall feeling was that *Mary and Rhoda* was an enjoyable blast from the past.

The bump received from the airing of *Mary and Rhoda* seemed to resonate with casting directors who seemed to get that Moore, with age, had gone from a quite solid leading lady to an equally effective character actress. Consequently, before the end of 2000, she would do good work in the little seen movies *Labor Pains* and *Good as Gold.*

During this period, Moore would occasionally reengage her defiant streak and actively go in search of the anti Mary Richards role, something that would cast the actress in a totally contrary role that would have her staunchest supporters scratching their heads. She would find such a role in 2001 when she heard that CBS was casting a down and dirty little crime thriller, *Like Mother, Like Son: The Strange Story of Sante and Kenny Kimes*, a truly lurid tale of mother and son criminals who graduate from small time cons and swindles to murder. This ripped from the headlines true story seemed to appeal to Moore's dark side and, she would hint during the promotion of the movie that the character of Sante and she may, by turns, have come from the same place, psychologically. These days, Moore rarely auditioned or went looking for roles but, as she would recall during a press tour interview with *People*, in this case she made an exception.

"I called CBS and said I want to play this role," she related. Moore showed how serious she was when she delved deep into the character, spending time in Riker's Island where the real Sante spent her last years and thoroughly researching the case and the psychology of sociopaths. Moore became fascinated with the case and the notion that she would be playing a character whose criminality was molded by childhood abuse and the exploitation of several men. "This stuff fascinates me," she told *People*. "It makes you wonder about people you know."

During filming, it became evident that Moore was quite good at exhibiting menace and no small amount of tension with a look or a matter of fact sense of menace. But Moore was almost giddy as she explained her descent to the dark side. "You will see an all new Mary in this movie. I wear very low cut dresses and the type of undergarments Julia Roberts wore in *Erin Brockovich*.

Sadly, *Like Mother, Like Son: The Strange Story of Sante and Kenny Kimes* suffered the same fate as much of Moore's later work, a television movie that received mixed reviews (although Moore was applauded for her ability to put viewers on the edge of their seats) and a quick disappearance from even her most loyal fans' memory.

The next couple of years saw Moore in a state of bliss.

She seemed content to spend quality and largely quiet time with her husband and a tight knit circle of friends. There seemed no real rhyme or reason to the work she did over the next couple of years. If it sounded like fun and had interesting people in it, Moore was seemingly on board.

There was the guest shot in an episode of *The Ellen (DeGeneres) Show*, the role of a tyrannical high school principal in the teen comedy *Cheats* which went on to near oblivion after a promised theatrical release was canceled at the last minute and the television movie *Miss Lettie and Me,* opposite Burt Reynolds, in which Moore played an isolated old lady who comes around just in time for the holidays.

Moore seemed comfortable with her life. She had come to terms with her diabetes and her own mortality. It had been a roller coaster life. Now closing in on 70, Moore was playing it day by day.

Chapter Twenty-Six
When in Doubt: Dick

Dick Van Dyke was easily Moore's most endearing and loving relationship. He had been in her life for decades, always supportive and always encouraging and, as history had seen, always there with an idea that would literally jumpstart her career. And by 2002, Moore seemed poised for another helping hand.

She had been working at her leisure, yet fairly consistently, on a number of divergent projects. Going on 65, she was content on many fronts. But there seemed to be something gnawing at her psyche. Moore was doing good work, often times better than the material, and had emerged as a competent to very good character player in her later years. But she had reached a point where, by 2002, she was just…well…looking for that 'something.' Truth be known, Moore was beginning to sense impending mortality and was, by association, anxious to go out doing good work that would also be fun.

That's when Moore received a phone call from Van Dyke. He had been offered a part that was quite special. But he was not ready to do it without her. Moore and Van Dyke had had a nodding acquaintance with *The Gin Game* since its theater premiere in 1977. Van Dyke was a particularly strong advocate for the power of the play and would often recommend that Moore and he do the play together before they would laughingly agree to do it when they were old enough to believably play the parts.

With Van Dyke's call, both finally felt it was time. The film version of *The Gin Game*, which would be produced in conjunction with PBS, would be true to the original premise of the play, two elderly residents of a senior center home, meet and, through a series of card games, draws dramatic, unsympathetic and often profane pictures as the pair digs deep into each other's hopes, fears and anger.

Moore readily accepted her old friend's invitation and realized that this would not be the ideal fix for those who had followed her career and had preconceived nostalgic notions. "There is such a tremendous fondness for both of us," she told *The Los Angeles Times*. "I think this adds so much to this play. I hope the audience is prepared for this. It's not a light comedy, because, toward the end, you see these people reveal more and more about themselves and how twisted they are."

That Van Dyke would acknowledge that "*The Gin Game* was such a labor of love and we wanted to do it together" was near understatement. From the moment filming commenced, Moore and Van Dyke were the centerpiece of a literal love fest. Between set ups of the most emotionally demanding scenes, Moore and Van Dyke would often break into spontaneous song. It was clear to even the most casual observer that the magic between the pair was still there.

Moore was at a loss to explain the chemistry between them. "I don't know how to explain it," she told *The Los Angeles Times*. "We are just Dick and Mary."

However, one wanted to couch it, the chemistry present on *The Gin Game* set was palpable and often the by-product of humor and good cheer. A prime example was the scene in which Van Dyke's character calls Moore a bitch. It was an emotional moment that played tough and wrenching in the final cut of the film. But what happened after the take was anything but. Moore immediately broke the tension when she matter-of-factly said "You've been wanting to call me that for years."

Moore kept the old age makeup and her dramatic edge in her follow up project, yet another television movie called *Blessings* in which an aging estate owner and a kind hearted handy man join forces for different reasons when a baby is abandoned literally on their doorstep. Things take an unexpected turn when the baby's parents turn up. A happy ending and yet another excuse for Moore to play against her own type make this a worth watching item if you can find it.

Shortly after completing *Blessings*, Moore once again heard from Van Dyke and, by association CBS, to return to the nostalgic world of Rob and Laura Petrie in a one-hour television special entitled *The Dick Van Dyke Show Revisited.* The premise, in which Rob and Sally are asked to write a comic eulogy for their old boss, and features several original cast members including Van Dyke and Moore (with several by now deceased actors appearing in grainy archival footage) came across as a bit awkward and dated but ultimately delivered the goods for those into the nostalgic quality of it all. For Moore, in particular, it was a chance to catch up and reminisce with old friends from the show. Moore had reached a point in her life and career where looking back was not so painful.

The roles she would take between 2005-2008 were nondescript at best. She played a small role in the 2005 television movie *Snow Wonder*, guested in a three-episode story arc on *That 70's Show* and guest starred in two episodes of the Brooke Shields top lining series *Lipstick Jungle*. Surprisingly, there seemed to be little in the way of offers for theatrical films. Why is not certain. Moore still carried some cache from *Ordinary People* and some of her smaller movies. Part of the reason may well have been that her health and long weeks in far-flung locations did not allow her to stray far from home. Truth be known, Moore might well have not wanted to work that hard anymore.

The next three years saw Moore working less on her career and more on the philosophical and yes, spiritual aspects of her life. She felt confident in surviving a myriad of personal and professional challenges to pen a second autobiography and to step up her charity work and lobbying on behalf of diabetes and the humane treatment of animals. Moore was encouraged about the success she appeared to be having in humanitarian causes. And she was realistic enough to know that the ravages of diabetes were closing in.

Chapter Twenty-Seven
Do Not Go Gentle

The much-vaunted 'fourth wave' in the evolution of feminism, which most experts peg as beginning in 2008, would reach its apex in 2009, making strides as a culmination of technology, politics and psychology.

Among the movement's most notable victories were Sonia Sotomayor's confirmation to the Supreme Court of The United States by a 68-31 vote on August 6, 2009. It was also the year that five women (Elizabeth Blackburn and Carol Greider for medicine, Herta Muller for literature, Elinor Ostrom for economics and Ada Yonath for chemistry) would all win the Nobel Prize. On August 15, 2009, *The New York Times* would boast the headline "G.I. Jane" and a massive article on women's increased combat role in the military. Of near equal significance, the Reverend Mary Douglas Glasspool was confirmed as the bishop of the diocese of Los Angeles.

Moore was spending the year 2009 marking a moment in time all her own. She was appearing in a fairly minor role in a very minor film called *Against the Current*. It would be the actress's very last movie. But that did not mean that she would not been seen or heard.

Two-thousand and nine would be the year when Moore would give an impassioned speech to Congress to request an increase in funding for diabetes research. By this time, Moore had become a practiced hand at slicing through the politics of the issue and, often citing her own battles as well as many other 'real people' who were dealing with the disease, including many professional athletes and, yes, politicians. She found many of the country's decision makers amenable to giving diabetes funding a much closer look.

Moore was also hard at work on her second autobiography *Growing Up Again: Life, Loves and Oh Yeah, Diabetes.* Unlike her first memoir, *After All*, Moore now had the benefit of more life experiences as well as the attitude of just laying it out there with no frills attached to make *Growing Up Again*, with an emphasis to her battles with diabetes, a substantial adjunct to her previous book.

Moore would do extensive press for *Growing Up Again* and, in the process, would often wax philosophical about her life and the myriad personal challenges she had faced. She told *CNN* interviewer Larry King "I don't think there's a person on earth who hasn't had as much pain as I have." But, in a *New York Times* interview she did count herself lucky. "I've been a diabetic for about 35 years now and I'm one of the lucky ones who has managed to live that long without having major problems."

Moore's statement was extreme understatement. The reality was that well into the 2000's, Moore was regularly victimized by the inevitable onset of diabetes's later stages. When out in public, Moore now appeared extremely gaunt and frail. Her equilibrium and steadily failing vision made even walking around her home an adventure. In both the *New York Times* and *CNN* interviews, Moore matter-of-factly conceded that she was beginning to have problems. "I do have problems with my eyes and if I fall I generally break a bone."

But Moore refused to give up.

Although diabetes had left her a veritable shell of herself in terms of health and emotional well-being, there was still that fighting spirit. One that said she could still get up in front of a camera and perform. More than one person in her close circle was thus surprised when she agreed to appear opposite her old *Mary Tyler Moore Show* friend Betty White in the sitcom *Hot in Cleveland* in which White's character ends up in jail for hiding stolen property and finds that Moore is her cellmate. It was the classic case of cast and crew pulling together in every possible way to make Moore's stint on the set as easy as possible and, by all accounts, Moore, ever the trooper, was able to pull it off.

Show producer Todd Milliner had been a lifelong fan of the actress and, in a conversation with *Entertainment Weekly*, admitted to being a bit fearful at meeting her. "I had to summon the courage to walk downstairs to say hello before the table read. I figured she'd just say hi, say get the hell out of here and then chuck a hat at me. I couldn't have been more wrong. She invited me into the dressing room. She was so kind. We sat together and had as normal a conversation as I could at the moment. She kept me there for a half hour. It was one of the best half hours of my life."

Moore by 2010 was forthright in explaining what

was going on with her ongoing battle with diabetes. Contrary to the speculation and rumors that had surrounded her deteriorating state, she claimed that she was not blind but that the disease had affected her peripheral vision and that she could navigate across rooms in her home.

But with Moore now rarely seen in public and her work having essentially stopped, the rumors persisted. These rumors caught fire when it was announced that, in 2011, Moore had undergone brain surgery to remove a benign tumor from the lining tissue of her brain. Doctors insisted that it was simply a precautionary procedure and that the tumor had not been malignant.

But this precautionary procedure would be a contributing factor in her seemingly rapid decline following the surgery. According to reports in the *Daily Mail* and other media outlets, Moore had been proscribed medication after the surgery which resulted in the actress suffering hallucinations and bouts of confusion. Which, by 2012, was resulting in regular emotional outbursts and conflicts with her husband which, in turn, resulted in visits from emergency medical units and the eventual public revelation that Moore's health was seemingly in rapid decline.

By 2012, Moore's mobility had declined to the point where she was often confined to a wheelchair. She was also, reportedly, suffering heart and kidney problems. The actress was pretty much confined to her home at that point but still managed to keep in touch with her close friends by telephone. Sadly, the conversations, while welcomed by her friends, were not encouraging.

In an article in *The Closer*, quoted by *The Washington Post*, Betty White acknowledged that "her eyesight is one of the big problems right now. She is almost beyond the point of being able to see." In the same article, Dick Van Dyke reported that "I don't see her often but I talk to her a bunch. She hasn't been too well. She's really having a battle with it, I'm sorry to say."

Moore's husband would remain the one constant in her life as the disease continued to wrack her body. Levine was constantly by her side, bravely dealing with the negative side effects of diabetes and being a constant at her bedside, doing what he could as both a doctor and a loving husband to ease her suffering. But it was not always easy.

Family friend Dr. Mark Atkinson, in a *New York Post* story, recalled that he would be in touch with Levine on a regular basis regarding Moore's progress. "I would keep in touch with Levine. We laughed together. We cried together. We were disappointed together."

It seemed almost a certainty that, in her weakened state, Moore's acting career was over. But behind the scenes, the positive response to Moore's last appearance on *Hot in Cleveland* had set the wheels in motion for Moore to make a return appearance. An appearance that had started with the sad news that Moore's longtime friend and Mary Tyler Moore co-star Valerie Harper had announced that she had terminal brain cancer and, according to reports, had only a few months to live (although she would show marked improvement in the ensuing months).

Producer Milliner was saddened at the news but

saw a way to turn the situation into a positive. "We had always wanted Mary back on the show because we had such a blast the first time. But this [Harper's illness] lit a fire and we set out to get it done."

For a storyline that brought the show's bowling team back together, Milliner found immediate enthusiasm from the women of *Hot in Cleveland* who had also been regulars on *The Mary Tyler Moore Show* (Betty White, Georgia Engel) and Cloris Leachman were thrilled to be part of getting the old gang back together. The producer recalled that word of the episode and, most excitedly, that Moore would be back to be part of it spread through Hollywood. A packed to the rafters press conference fueled the partly nostalgic/part melancholy interest. The consensus, in hushed tones around Hollywood, was that Moore did not have a whole lot of time left and that this, truly, could be her last acting role.

Milliner recalled the warmth and nostalgia of that moment in a conversation with *Entertainment Weekly*.

"Mary didn't really give notes on the character or her scene in a restaurant. The most significant memory I have of that night was watching her watch her friends. In a great way, she seemed to get a little lost in the moment. The reunion was very important to her. She'd be watching the other ladies perform and then say, 'Oh yeah, I've got lines here.' And we'd all laugh."

Audience tickets for that episode were at a premium and Milliner took great pains to prolong the suspense. "When it came time for the taping, we blocked the set from the audience so they could not see Mary sitting at the table. When we removed it, the standing ovation and the roar of the crowd was overwhelming. It went on forever and Mary started to tear up. The episode was called 'Love Is All Around'…

"And it really was that night."

After what would be her final acting credit, Moore retreated into isolation. Between 2013 and 2015, emergency medical technicians were called to Moore's house on at least a dozen occasions to deal with emergency situations caused by her diabetes or the side effects of medication. Although it would never be completely confirmed, Moore, during this period, was beginning to exhibit signs of Alzheimer's' disease. These latest setbacks led her husband and others to consider putting Moore into an assisted living facility. However, Moore insisted that she be allowed to stay in her home and nobody would argue with her.

Moore and ex-husband, Tinker, kept in touch through the years and, consequently, were well aware of each other's lives and their respective declining health. Grant Tinker died on November 28, 2016 at the age of 90. Moore was despondent over the fact that yet another link to her past life had passed.

In a prepared statement, Moore offered that "I am deeply saddened to learn that my former husband and professional mentor Grant Tinker has passed away. I am forever grateful and proud of what we have achieved together. Grant was a brilliant, driven executive."

This would be the last statement from the actress. Moore retreated into silence. Moore was a realist. She knew in her soul that time was running out.

Chapter Twenty-Eight
Into That Good Night

And so it seemed did those around her.

In her declining days, Moore was nothing if not consistent in keeping in close contact with her close friends via telephone. And although she tried to keep up a good front, it was evident that she was quickly fading.

Rose Marie, her comedic partner in crime on *The Dick Van Dyke Show*, related to Radar OnLine.com that her phone calls with Moore told her a lot in those last days. "She suffered so much in those last few years. She had a tumor and she had diabetes and she was going blind and she couldn't hear very well. When I talked with her at the end it was always about the good old days and all the fun we had. But you could tell that she sounded very sick."

Marie's worst fears were confirmed the night she received a phone call from Van Dyke who had just gotten off the phone with Moore. "He called me and said, 'It's very bad. She's going to go very soon now.'"

Dorothy Sepe, who had been the family cook for 14 years, echoed those comments when she told Radaronline.com about Moore's final weeks. "She was in pain and had a host of medical issues. Her eyesight was going, she had bad feet, her body was basically failing her." Sepe further offered that Moore's physical problems were compounded by a lingering, deep-rooted sense of guilt about the death of her son. "She never got over the death of Richie. It just broke her heart."

Ever the devoted husband, Levine's anguish and exhaustion in having to literally be on call as Moore's life ebbed was palpable. Moore's illness had finally called for the actress to be in a 24-hour hospice situation, with people there to attend to her every needs. While not in a vegetative state, Moore's myriad of illnesses, including Alzheimer's had reduced her to a noncommunicative situation. Which left Levine to handle all communications with other doctors and close family friends.

By the first of January, most of Levine's calls were to close friends with progress reports on Moore's declining health and the dire prediction that if they wanted to see Moore, they should probably do it soon. Valerie Harper was one of those who received such a call as she related in a Facebook message. "Last week, to prepare me, I was kindly warned by Mary Tyler Moore's dear husband, Dr. Robert Levine, that she was in the very last stages of life."

Carl Reiner would recall with much pain his communication with Levine mere days before her passing in a conversation with *Entertainment Tonight*. "I spoke to her husband the day or so before she passed away. I remember telling him that she may not remember him but to whisper in her ear that it was okay to go."

What Moore was in the throes of during those

final days was a compendium of maladies that were combing to make her last days a painful ordeal. In medical terms...Aspirational pneumonia, the many long-term effects of diabetes and hypoxia (a lack of oxygen in her tissues). Add the reported psychological damage, much of which allegedly attributed to her ongoing guilt over the death of her son, and it was no wonder that many of those close to her at the end of her life, felt that she was ready to die.

By January 19, 2017, Moore's health had been downgraded to 'grave.' Moore was immediately transferred to a hospital in Greenwich, Connecticut where she was put on a respirator to facilitate her breathing. Over the next week, Levine, with the aid of other attending physicians, contemplated taking Moore off of life support. On Tuesday night, January 24, the decision was made to remove Moore from life support and to let nature take its course. But rather than go quietly during the night, Moore lingered well into the next morning while her condition remained grave. Family members began to trickle into the hospital that day to pay their last respects and, most tellingly,...

...To say their final goodbyes.

Moore took her final labored breaths at 2:15 p.m. on Wednesday January 25 and, with Levine and close family and friends at her bedside, went to her final reward.

Chapter Twenty-Nine
Rest in Peace

Peoria, Illinois resident Debra Capperrune took the announcement of Mary Tyler Moore's death real hard. "I cried for two days and then I said 'let's go,'" she related to The *Connecticut Post*. Capperrune drove 15 hours for the sole purpose of attending Moore's funeral. "I didn't stop. I drove straight through."

Capperrune drove up to the entrance to the Oak Lawn Cemetery in Fairfield on Sunday, January 29 shortly before the announced 11 a.m. start of the service. The Oak Lawn Cemetery was a well-known, serene final resting place, reportedly consisting of more than 100 acres and the final interment spot for an estimated 23,000 people that included such notables as actor Jason Robards, Negro League baseball player Rufus Baker and World War II Medal of Honor winner Michael J. Daly.

Capperrune was surprised and somewhat disappointed to find a line of local police officers standing at the entrance who explained that the service was private and that only a select number of family and friends would be allowed in. "I didn't know the funeral was closed," said Capperrune. "But it was okay. I just wanted to come and pay tribute to her. I knew I had to get there."

It was a brisk 40 degrees, made even more so by the intermittent winds that blew through Oak Lawn as a line of cars made their way through the cemetery gates and up to the small white chapel where a very brief service would commence. The mood was somber. Levine was, reportedly, showing the strain of the previous days on his face as he greeted close friends and family members as they walked into the chapel. After the service, the group repaired to Moore's burial site.

The family had made a grand effort to project an emotion of peace and serenity at the burial site. The burial mound was covered with white orchids and roses. A stone angel gazed out over the site, backed by a newly planted row of white birch trees. According to several news reports, the family had reportedly purchased a dozen burial plots that surrounded Moore's grave for the purpose of giving the actress everlasting peace and privacy in the afterlife.

Moore's family knew the impact the actress had on countless millions and so, after the conclusion of the private ceremony, they opened up the cemetery to the public to come in and have a private moment with their beloved Mary.

"I grew up with her and I loved her," Capperrune told *The Connecticut Post*. "I must have played 'Love Is All Around' a thousand times since her death."

In the days that followed, tribute to the actress cam in from the celebrity world as well as the blue collar working world. No matter their station in life, their expressions of condolence and joyous memories had one thing in common.

They were sad for the loss and consoled by the

memory of what Mary Tyler Moore had meant to them. Perhaps no one was finally sum it up more eloquently than Levine who had spent 33 years with the love of his life.

"I can't believe she is gone. Mary was my life, my light my love. The emptiness I feel without her with me is without bottom. She was a force of nature who fiercely defended her autonomy even as her health was failing. Mary was fearless, determined and willful. If she felt strongly about something or there was a truth to be told she would do it, no matter the consequences. She was kind, genuine, approachable honest and humble. And she had that smile. Oh to see her smile, that smile just once more. My sadness is only tempered by the remarkable outpouring of good wishes, tributes and personal 'Mary stories' told with heart touched by her grace.

"As long as we all remember her, talk about her, share our stories about her and what she meant to us, her light will never go out."

Epilogue
Life and the Statue

To many, it was just too ironic and, perhaps, a bit supernatural. One of those twists of the tale that are the hallmarks of such classic storytellers as O'Henry, Rod Serling and Robert Bloch.

Two days after Moore's passing, Gwendolyn Gillen, the Milwaukee sculptor who had created the bronze statue of Mary Richards in her classic throwing her hat in the air pose that has delighted countless visitors and residents of Minneapolis alike since its unveiling in 2002, also passed away. He passing was quiet and with little notoriety in a Madison, Wisconsin Hospice, effectively completing the connection the two women had in life, as she followed Moore very quickly into the next life.

The story of the statue, its creator and Moore being psychically joined at the hip seemed perfect. And a fantasy to finally hang Moore's trademark hat on.

According to Pop History Dig.com, It began early in 2000 when the cable channel *TV Land*, which had made its bones and a massive viewership by showing endless reruns of timeless television classics, came to

Minneapolis with the idea of commemorating *The Mary Tyler Moore* Show and, by association, Moore herself with a statue placed lovingly in a location that had been memorialized by the show. In preparation, *TV Land* had solicited conceptual ideas from more than 20 artists and had awarded the job of a lifetime to regionally known Milwaukee sculptor Gwendolyn Gillen.

Gillen, working in conjunction with *TV Land*, came up with the ideal nod to Moore and the show, an eight foot tall bronze of an exuberant Mary Richards tossing her trademark Tam O' Shatner hat into the air. The sculptor, not surprisingly a committed fan of Moore and the show, saw the importance of presenting both joy and determination in the piece as she explained to *The Minneapolis Star Tribune*.

"She [Moore] helped break the stereotype of womanhood that our generation grew up believing was our destiny. She was the light breeze that blew through our minds and left us with the feeling that we could do anything we wanted to."

The concept seemed to work in the hearts and minds of Minneapolis residents and local politicians when presented her design to the city in early 2001. The response was largely enthusiastic. But there were some doubters. Tim Connolly of the publication *Minneapolis Issues* wanted to know "Why is *TV Land* putting up this statue? If it is marketing and the mayor is buying into it, then we are complicit in marketing the *TV Land Network*." Professor Clay Steinman echoed Connolly's concerns when he "likened the statue to honoring a unicorn. It's honoring something that doesn't exist." After some spirited, mildly contentious back and forth, the Mary Tyler Moore project went forward.

On May 8, 2002, the statue was unveiled on a 43 degree morning in front of an enthusiastic crowd of approximately 3,000. Playing in the background during the unveiling was a live rendition of the song 'Love is All Around.' But what would ultimately make the moment was that Moore had come to the ceremony to offer support and to help foster the spirit of nostalgia and goodwill in the moment.

Moore delighted the crowd with her humor and good cheer, eliciting waves of laughter when she recited some of her classic television lines like 'Ooohh Rob!' and 'Mr. Grant!' in that trademark little girl trembling tone.

The statue would become an instant tourist attraction, drawing people both locally and from across the country to snap photos, pose in front of the statue and just have a good natured giggle at the memories of what Moore and *The Mary Tyler Moore Show* had meant in their lives. It would stay at that location until 2015 when a renovation of the area where the statue stood necessitated it being moved indoors to the city's Crystal Court Visitors Center.

While people still sought out the statue, the whole experience did not have the same feel and so people would literally count the weeks and months until the renovation was completed in 2017 and the statue was moved back to its original place of honor.

The crowds' return in even larger numbers than before was expected. It was as if Mary Richards had once again come home. Moore died on January 25, 2017 and it was as if the world had suddenly stopped.

Especially in Minneapolis. People gathered at the statue, laying flowers at its base and shedding tears that their Mary was gone. The sadness was deepened when the statue's creator passed away two days later.

But the memories centering around Gillen's ability to bring everything that people loved about Mary and what she represented into her work could not be denied. Nor would the power of goodness and determination that Moore and her career had left to the generations of women to come ever go away.

When pressed over the years, Moore would concede that there was a sense of taking what she had done and passing it on to the coming generations. There was a real sense of her place in time and what she would ultimately pass along.

Moore said as much when she was present at the unveiling of her likeness at the 2002 presentation of her statue in Minneapolis.

"I hope when a little girl walks by the statue, she will ask her mother who that was and that it will be explained to her that she was a young woman who had a dream and followed it through."

APPENDIX

AWARDS AND NOMINATIONS

1963

Nominated for an Emmy Award for Outstanding Lead Actress in a Comedy Series for *The Dick Van Dyke Show*.

1964

Won an Emmy Award for Outstanding Lead Actress in a Comedy Series for *The Dick Van Dyke Show*.

1965

Won a Golden Globes Award for Outstanding Actress in a Television Series for *The Dick Van Dyke Show*.

1966

Won an Emmy Award for Outstanding Lead Actress in a Comedy Series for *The Dick Van Dyke Show*.

1971

Won a Golden Globes Award for Outstanding Actress in a Television Series for *The Mary Tyler Moore Show*.

Nominated for an Emmy Award for Outstanding Lead Actress in a Comedy Series for *The Mary Tyler Moore Show*.

1972

Nominated for an Emmy Award for Outstanding

Lead Actress in a Comedy Series for *The Mary Tyler Moore Show.*

Nominated for a Golden Globes Award for Best Actress in a Television Series for *The Mary Tyler Moore Show.*

1973

Won an Emmy Award for Outstanding Lead Actress in a Comedy Series for *The Mary Tyler Moore Show.*

1974

Won an Emmy Award for Outstanding Lead Actress in a Comedy Series for *The Mary Tyler Moore Show.*

1975

Nominated for an Emmy Award for Outstanding Lead Actress in a Comedy Series for *The Mary Tyler Moore Show.*

1976

Won an Emmy Award for Outstanding Lead Actress in a Comedy Series for *The Mary Tyler Moore Show.*

1977

Nominated for an Emmy Award for Outstanding Lead Actress in a Comedy Series for *The Mary Tyler Moore Show.*

1980

Won Golden Globes Award for Best Actress in a Motion Picture Drama for *Ordinary People.*

Won a Tony Awards' Award Special Award for *Whose Life is it Anyway?*

Nominated for Academy Award for Best Actress in a Motion Picture for *Ordinary People.*

Nominated for a Drama Desk Award for

Outstanding Actress in a Play for *Whose Life is it Anyway?*

1985

Won Tony Awards' Award for Best Reproduction (play or musical) for *Joe Egg.*

Won the Women in Film Crystal Award.

1993

Won an Emmy Award for Outstanding Supporting Actress in a Limited Series or Movie for *Stolen Babies.*

MARY TYLER MOORE TRIVIA

Mary Tyler Moore auditioned for the role of Annie in the movie version of the Stephen King novel *Misery*. The role ultimately went to Kathy Bates. Very early in her career, Moore went up for the role of Jennifer North in the movie *Valley of the Dolls*. She lost the role to Sharon Tate.

But Moore was definitely up to the task in *Ordinary People* where she beat out legendary actresses Ann Margaret, Lee Remick and Natalie Wood for the coveted starring role.

Mary Tyler Moore dated, for real, her co-star Ed Asner shortly after her divorce from Grant Tinker. Asner admitted the date to *Vanity Fair*. "We'll call it a momentary lapse of judgment on her part," he joked. "But I was quite honored. Of the date itself, Asner would only say "We were just too close for comfort so I retreated into my comedic self and let the boys have at her."

Mary Tyler Moore received a star on the Hollywood Walk of Fame on September 8, 1992. Her star is located at 7021 Hollywood Boulevard.

At one point in her life, Mary Tyler Moore smoked as many as 60 cigarettes a day.

And speaking of cigarettes, Kent Cigarettes was an early sponsor of *The Dick Van Dyke Show* and would regularly give free cartons of their cigarettes to the cast and crew. Moore did not like Kents and would always take her share of the cartons and trade them in at a local store for a brand she preferred.

Moore was once mentioned by name by the character Snoopy in a Peanuts newspaper comic strip.

Moore was a descendent of Civil War notable Lt. Colonel Lewis T. Moore.

Mary Tyler Moore was awarded the Golden Turkey Award for the Worst Performance by and Actor or Actress as a clergyman or a nun for her turn in the movie *Change of Habi*t. Moore said she was thrilled to get it.

The Mary Tyler Moore Show was the first scripted show in television history to use the word 'gay." It was uttered in the episode "My Brother's Keeper."

Sonny Curtis, the singer/songwriter who penned *The Mary Tyler Moore Show* theme song, "Love Is All Around," was once a member of the band Buddy Holly & The Crickets. Curtis is also responsible for that classic rock song "I Fought The Law."

Mary Tyler Moore directed one episode of her show. It was the season five episode entitled "A Boy's Best Friend."

The Mary Tyler Moore Enterprises logo featured the meowing kitten. The kitten was found at a Minneapolis animal shelter. The kitten was named Mimsie. After the show concluded, a crew member adopted Mimsie who would go on to live to the ripe old age of 20.

During the casting process for the character of Ted Baxter, the leading candidates for the role were actors Lyle Waggoner and John Aniston. Waggoner, who was at the time a regular on *The Carol Burnett Show*, was hesitant to leave his regular gig for the untested *The Mary Tyler Moore Show* and so passed. Aniston, the father of Jenifer Aniston and a long time regular on the soap opera *Days of Our Lives,* was called back to audition twice before the producers decided that he was just not the type they were looking for.

Hazel Frederick was seen in every single episode of *The Mary Tyler Moore Show*. Who was Hazel Frederick you ask? Well Hazel was a local Minneapolis resident who happened to be out and about, shopping. Packages in hand, Hazel was walking down the street, minding her own business, when she happened to step right behind Moore and into the shot where Mary throws her hat into the air. Consequently, if you look at the opening montage, you'll spot Hazel looking askance at the spectacle where she would remain for the ages.

The Mary Tyler Moore Show was the first US television network series to break character and to feature a curtain call in front of a live audience. It occurred during the final episode of the series when Moore stepped to stage front and introduced her castmates just before the end credits rolled for the last time.

At one point early in the show's existence, *The Mary Tyler Moore Show* was in danger of being cancelled. So much so that the producers came up with an alternative ending to the show that, if used, would have sent the series out with a literal bang. As the story played out, a mad bomber was leaving bombs all over the city of Minneapolis. It was determined that the bomber was actually somebody who worked in the WJM newsroom. Chaos would have ensued as the cast began to suspect each other. At the end of the never-used storyline, it was determined that the bomber was one of the nameless, faceless people we always saw working in the background on the newsroom set.

SOURCES

INTERVIEWS

I would like to thank the following people for generously giving of their time and memories--Jennifer Keishin Armstrong, Randall Munson, Virginia Carter.

BOOKS

After All by Mary Tyler Moore. Putnam (1995). *Growing Up Again: Life, Loves and Oh Yeah, Diabetes* by Mary Tyler Moore. St. Martins (2009). *Mary Tyler Moore* by Jason Bonderoff. St. Martins (1986). *Mary and Lou and Rhoda and Ted and All the Brilliant Minds Who Made The Mary Tyler Moore Show a Classic* by Jennifer Keishin Armstrong. Simon & Schuster (2013). *The Dick Van Dyke Show Book: The Definitive History of Television's Most Enduring Comedy* by Vince Waldron and Dick Van Dyke. Chicago Review Press (2011). *My Lucky Life In and Out of Show Business* by Dick Van Dyke. Three Rivers Press (2012).

NEWSPAPERS

Variety, The Brooklyn Daily Eagle, USA Today, Washington Post, Baltimore Sun, Los Angeles Times, Toronto Sun, Ottawa Citizen, The Hollywood Reporter, New York Post, New York Daily News, Associated Press, Minneapolis Star Tribune, United

Press International, The National Ledger, The Sunday Times, New York Times, Connecticut Post,

MAGAZINES

TV Guide, Ms. Magazine, Parade, Rolling Stone, Town and Country Magazine, Entertainment Weekly, Emmy Magazine, Esquire, The Federalist, People, Time, Interview, McCall's, Closer

WEBSITES

Salon.com, American Television.com, AOL.com, Neatorama.com, Revelist.com, Yahoocelebrity.com, Radaronline.com, Pop History Dig.co, Infoplease.com, National Women's History Project.org, The Women's Rights Movement in the US aolnews.com, The Second Wave of Women's Feminism wikpedia.com. The National Organization of Women.com.

TELEVISION

Charlie Rose Interview, Oprah Winfrey Interview, CBS News, ABC News, CNN, Fox News,

RADIO

National Public Radio,

MISCELLANEOUS

Barbara Walters interview, Screen Actor's Guild Lifetime Achievement Award Speech, Archives Of American Television, Marilyn Beck Interview, Valerie Harper's Facebook message, Robert Levine personal statement,

About the Author

New York Times bestselling author Marc Shapiro has written more than 60 nonfiction celebrity biographies, more than two-dozen comic books, numerous short stories and poetry, and three short form screenplays. He is also a veteran freelance entertainment journalist.
His young adult book *JK Rowling: The Wizard Behind Harry Potter* was on *The New York Times* bestseller list for four straight weeks. His fact-based book *Total Titanic* was also on *The Los Angeles Times* bestseller list for four weeks. *Justin Bieber: The Fever* was on the nationwide Canadian bestseller list for several weeks.

Shapiro has written books on such personalities as Shonda Rhimes, George Harrison, Carlos Santana, Annette Funicello, Lorde, Lindsay Johan, E.L. James, Jamie Dornan, Dakota Johnson, Adele and countless others. He also co-authored the autobiography of mixed martial arts fighter Tito Ortiz, *This Is Gonna Hurt: The Life of a Mixed Martial Arts Champion.*

He is currently working on a biography of Lin-Manuel Miranda as well as updating his biographies of Gillian Anderson and Lucy Lawless for Riverdale Avenue Books.

Other Riverdale Avenue Books Titles by Marc Shapiro

What is Hip? The Life and Times of The Tragically Hip

Hey Joe: The Unauthorized Biography of a Rock Classic

Trump This! The Life and Times of Donald Trump, An Unauthorized Biography

The Secret Life of EL James

The Real Steele: The Unauthorized Biography of Dakota Johnson

Inside Grey's Anatomy: The Unauthorized Biography of Jamie Dornan

Annette Funicello: America's Sweetheart

Game: The Resurrection of Tim Tebow

Legally Bieber: Justin Bieber at 18

Lindsay Lohan: Fully Loaded, From Disney to Disaster

Lorde: Your Heroine, How This Young Feminist Broke the Rules and Succeeded

We Love Jenni: An Unauthorized Biography

Who Is Katie Holmes? An Unauthorized Biography

Norman Reedus: True Tales of The Waking Dead's Zombie Hunter, An Unauthorized Biography

Welcome to Shondaland: An Unauthorized Biography of Shonda Rhimes

CPSIA information can be obtained
at www.ICGtesting.com
Printed in the USA
BVHW041836051119
562988BV00014B/457/P